Battleground Europe
BELGIUM - HOLLAND

WALCHEREN
OPERATION INFATUATE

Battleground Europe
BELGIUM - HOLLAND

WALCHEREN
OPERATION INFATUATE

Andrew Rawson

LEO COOPER

Published by 2003
LEO COOPER
an imprint of
Pen & Sword Books Limited
47 Church Street, Barnsley, South Yorkshire S70 2AS

Copyright © Andrew Rawson 2003

ISBN 0 85052 961 1

A CIP catalogue of this book is available
from the British Library

Printed by CPI UK

*For up-to-date information on other titles produced under the Leo Cooper
imprint, please telephone or write to:*
Pen & Sword Books Ltd, FREEPOST, 47 Church Street
Barnsley, South Yorkshire S70 2AS
Telephone 01226 734222

CONTENTS

Ooster of Dockhaven, code named Uncle Beach, was protected by a series of obstacles. H Houterman

ACKNOWLEDGEMENTS

Until 1994, I had never heard of Walcheren Island or Operation INFATUATE. Having toured large parts of North West Europe, including Normandy, the Ardennes and Arnhem, I thought that I had a wide knowledge of the campaigns of the Second World War. How wrong I was.

A phone call from a friend, Allan Rogers, started the interest in Walcheren Island, which has finally led to this book. Allan's grandfather, Les Moran, was going to Holland for the 50th anniversary of a battle I had, as yet, not heard of. Knowing that I had more than a passing interest in anything military, Allan enquired if I would like to accompany him.

A few weeks later we arrived in Vlissingen, or Flushing as many veterans call it, on Walcheren. The weekend of commemorative parades and memorial services passed quickly but what I will never forget is the informal chats I had with the veterans. Although the rest of the world seemed to have forgotten about Walcheren, they never had and never would. In Les' own words 'although I was involved in other actions during the war, none has the haunting pull on me that Walcheren always has'. Hopefully, this book will bring Operation INFATUATE a wider audience, an audience it deserves.

Many people have helped me during the writing of this book. Above all the writers of the unit diaries deserve remembering. They had to type or write their account of the battle under difficult circumstances, often recounting the loss of close friends. A number of regimental historians, Matthew Little of the Royal Marines Museum in Portsmouth, Lieutenant-Colonel Hogg of the King's Own Scottish Borderers Regimental Museum in Berwick upon Tweed and Mr Clarke of the Royal Scots Regimental Museum in Edinburgh Castle in particular, have assisted in my research.

Hans Houterman of Middelburg, Walcheren has been a tremendous help. Over the past twenty years he has managed to accumulate a comprehensive archive of documents and photographs relating to Walcheren in the Second World War. As part of his research he has managed to trace many of the survivors, both Allied and German, privately publishing ten works of his own in Dutch. My own search for information would have taken far longer and I would have missed certain items of interest without access to Mr Houterman's archive. He also proof read the manuscript, correcting many errors and bringing to my attention local aspects of the battle not covered in British sources.

I would also like to thank the team at Pen and Sword for their co-operation during the preparation of this book. Brigadier Henry Wilson, has provided many useful pieces of advice throughout the writing process. Meanwhile, Roni Wilkinson and the design team have managed to conjure this publication out of my collection of words and pictures. In many ways it is down to them that the *Battleground Europe* series of books are so stimulating.

I dedicate this book to the hundreds of men like Les Moran, many of them no longer with us, who defeated one of the strongest sections of the Atlantic Wall. I hope that my son Alex never has to face the same ordeals that those young men had to in November 1944.

ADVICE FOR VISITORS

As any seasoned traveller to the battlefields will tell you, forward planning is the key to a successful visit. Take time to read through the book before you visit to get a feel for the battle. You may also try and acquire some of the titles listed in the further reading section at the end of this book. Although there are only a handful of published accounts covering the battle in detail, this book is not intended to be an authoritative history. It will, however, give the reader an insight into what took place on Walcheren Island in November 1944.

A comprehensive car tour at the end of the book guides you around the important locations on Walcheren. A number of short walks are included; walking allows the visitor time to take in the surroundings and refer to the book at leisure.

Travelling to Walcheren

Two continental ports, Zeebrugge and Rotterdam, serve the area equally well and both are about two hours drive from Walcheren. Your choice of route will probably be dictated by your starting point in the UK and the availability of crossings.

The route from Zeebrugge

After leaving the docks follow signs for Heist and Knokke, heading east. At the far end of Knokke, four miles from the port, the road heads inland. After ten miles, on the approach to Maldegem, turn left sign posted for Zelate and Antwerp. After fifteen miles, turn left at Zelate, heading north into Holland. A tunnel, starting at Terneuzen, takes you under the Westerschelde, the estuary leading into Antwerp. The toll bar is at the northern end of the tunnel. Continue north joining the motor way after three miles near to the town of Goes. Middelburg and Vlissingen are ten and fifteen miles to the west respectively.

The route from Rotterdam

There are two ways of reaching Walcheren from Rotterdam docks. The inland route, the A29, passes through Rosendaal en route for Antwerp. You may wish to visit the Commonwealth War Graves Cemetery at Bergen-op-Zoom, where many of the casualties from Operation Infatuate are buried. Directions are given from Junction 26, the Heerle junction, at the end of the book. Middelburg is forty miles from Bergen, along the A58. Vlissingen is five miles beyond Middelburg.

The alternative route, across the islands, takes you over a series of spectacular bridges. The N59 joins the A58 motorway near Goes. Middelburg is ten miles to the west, along the A58.

Staying on Walcheren

Walcheren has become a popular holiday destination, a potential advantage for the visitors to the island. Accommodation is both varied and plentiful, ranging from luxurious seaside hotels to campsites. A list of places to stay would fill half this book and be out of date in a short time. If you prefer to book a place to stay before crossing the North Sea, you can either approach a local travel agent or conduct your own search on the internet. Using search words such as 'Walcheren' or 'Zeeland' brings up a host of booking suggestions. There is also an excellent website covering all aspects of the province, including tourist attractions if you intend to make the most of your visit; the only drawback is that many features are only given in Dutch.

If, however, you wish to take your chances or prefer to choose where you stay on its own merits, there is a simple way of finding suitable accommodation. Most of the towns and seaside villages have tourist information offices, capable of giving you

Walcheren beach.

assistance. They all possess illustrated lists of places to stay. Many of the staff speak excellent English, as indeed do most people in Holland, and they can help you choose a place to suit your needs. For a small charge (eight percent of the accommodation fee in 2002), they will book your accommodation for you. This usually works out at around £3 to £4 a night for a double or twin room. It does, however, take out a lot of the uncertainty associated with securing a room and having to wander around an unfamiliar town.

Thousands of holidaymakers from all over north west Europe travel to Walcheren during the summer months to take advantage of the endless beaches. Advance booking would be advisable if you intend to travel at the height of the holiday season to avoid disappointment. Understandably, the island is less frantic in the spring and autumn; but you will have to chance your luck with the weather. The North Sea can be particularly ferocious at times, making the dunes inhospitable to all but the hardiest traveller.

The anniversary of the landings, 1 November, is a busy time too, although not on the scale experienced by Normandy or Arnhem. Even so, ceremonies and parades draw the dwindling number of veterans and large numbers of onlookers back to Walcheren every year. The Dutch cherish their liberators and their camaraderie with the veterans has lasted for years.

Tourist information centres

Vlissingen, 3 Oude Markt - **0118 - 422190** *(by the church)*
Middelburg, 40 Nieuwe Burg - **0118 - 659900** *(close to the town hall)*
Zoutelande, 2 Bosweg - **0118 - 561818** *(at the south end, on the main road)*
Westkapelle, 69a Markt (in the centre of the village)

The following guidelines will give you some idea of what to expect in the principal towns and villages.

Vlissingen

Vlissingen, known as Flushing until recent years, is a small seaside town surrounded by the types of industry associated with a busy port. Parts of the old town and the harbour, have changed very little and the location of some of the war time

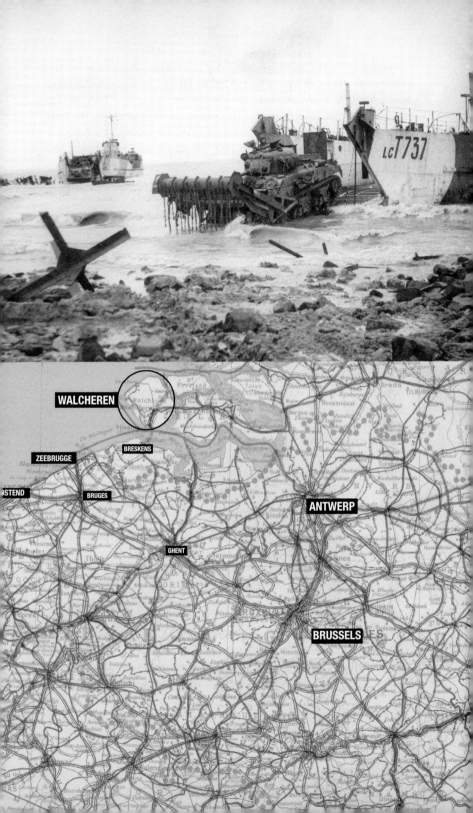

WALCHEREN

BRESKENS

ZEEBRUGGE

STEND

BRUGES

ANTWERP

GHENT

BRUSSELS

photographs are quite easy to trace. However, the battle for the town left many scars and large areas had to be rebuilt. Progress continues at a steady rate as Vlissingen struggles to keep up with the expansion in trade. The north end of the town, the new town, has grown immensely since the war. Even so, it is possible to trace the battle, with the help of many old buildings and features.

Although the layout of the docks has not changed, the wharves have been thoroughly modernised, making them impossible to visit. However, the ferry crossing to Breskens gives ample opportunity to study the battle for the quays and the railway station.

Zoutelande, Westkapelle and Domburg

The coastal resorts were the focus of heavy bombardments or fierce fighting and were completely rebuilt after the war. The villages have become attractive seaside resorts and although there has been some post war expansion, they have not been overrun with the type of attractions associated with some tourist resorts. The coastal town of Domburg on the north coast has many hotels and camping sites. Zoutelande, to the south west is also encircled by a number of camping sites, B & B's and caravan parks.

The resorts are protected from the offshore winds by huge sand dunes. Well-marked paths lead onto the beaches and there are many opportunities for a bracing walk along the coast.

Middelburg

Middelburg has retained many of its original features and large areas of the town look the same as they did sixty years ago. On the whole it escaped the ravages of war, saved from destruction by a remarkable series of incidents outlined later in the book. The main square hosts a regular market and it is dominated by a magnificent fifteenth century town hall. The abbey, with its huge bell tower is close by and well worth a visit. It houses a museum covering the history of Zeeland. Remains of the ancient moat surround part of the town and the canal, which passes close to the town centre, is a reminder how important water is on Walcheren.

Middelburg has a large shopping centre and it is possible to buy just about anything in the busy shopping malls. A large

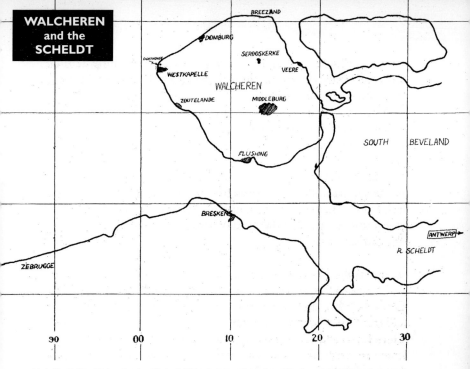

WALCHEREN and the SCHELDT

BREEZAND

DOMBURG

SEROOSKERKE

VEERE

LIGHTHOUSE

WESTKAPELLE

WALCHEREN

ZOUTELANDE

MIDDELBURG

SOUTH BEVELAND

FLUSHING

BRESKENS

ANTWERP

R. SCHELDT

ZEBRUGGE

90   00   10   20   30

Detail of the Schedle (or Scheldt) estuary, showing the key towns and villages

selection of cafés, bars and restaurants, catering for most tastes, can be found within walking distance of the main square.

Travelling around Walcheren

The island is quite easy to navigate around and you can rarely stray far from your intended destination. Middelburg Abbey's tower can be seen from many places and it can sometimes serve as a useful navigational aid if you happen to lose your bearings. You would be advised to buy a detailed map at one of the tourist information shops; some petrol stations also stock them. A compass can sometimes come in handy for finding your way around.

A car gives a traveller the flexibility to visit many places in a short space of time and sharing travelling costs with friends can make the journey relatively inexpensive. Driving on the right takes a little getting used to and it is quite easy to forget, particularly after a short stop on a quiet road. Drivers must remember to keep their eyes on the road, no matter how fascinating the surroundings are. If something of interest catches your eye, park your vehicle in a safe place so you can

13

study it in safety. One traffic rule in Holland takes a little getting used to. Bicycles have priority from the right at crossroads the same as motor vehicles.

The area is extremely flat and the only hills, as such, are the towering sand dunes on the coast. Those who are fit enough may choose to tour the battlefield by bicycle, a practical compromise. Holland is very friendly towards cyclists, and virtually every main road possesses a cycle-path. There are number of hire shops in all the towns and villages. Middelburg and Vlissingen railway stations provide a service costing about six Euros (around £3.50) for a day's hire. The deposit is 25 Euros (around £15) and you will need your passport for identification.

Walcheren has an excellent public transport system. A railway connection links Vlissingen and Middelburg with the mainland and the local bus network serves all the coastal villages on a regular basis.

I am afraid that if you have physical difficulty in getting around, the sand dunes are a serious obstacle. In almost every instance you have to climb fairly lengthy flights of steps to get onto the beach. Unfortunately, there are no alternatives in many cases.

High sand dunes protect the island from the sea.

CHAPTER ONE

THE NEED TO OPEN ANTWERP

As the month of August 1944 drew to a close, the Allies were sweeping across France and the Low Countries in full pursuit of the German Army. On 4 September, huge crowds met British troops as they entered the vital sea port of Antwerp. Although the city had been liberated without difficulty, little did the Allied generals know that it would take more than three months of hard fighting before the docks could be put to use. Rather than clearing the banks of the Schelde estuary of German troops, they turned their attentions to more tempting targets. It was a decision many would regret over the coming months.

As British and American spearheads advanced deeper across North-West Europe, Allied High Command was coming to terms with a new problem, supplies. Even as late as September the Allies had not managed to establish sufficient deep water facilities. Last ditch stands by Geman troops in Calais and Boulogne had reduced the docks to ruins and the majority of supplies were still being landed at the temporary harbours in

The docks at Antwerp with some undamaged Belgian and Dutch barges. However, this vital port could not be used until the banks of the Schelde estuary had been cleared of German forces.

Normandy. With winter only a few weeks away, the need for a sheltered port was becoming paramount.

Although 21st Army Group had secured the city of Antwerp, the port could not be used. Great steps had been taken to guard to entrance to the Schelde estuary with coastal batteries. Ships then had to navigate a thirty-kilometre length of water, bordered by enemy held territory and dotted with hundreds of mines. It would take all the attentions of the First Canadian Army to clear the Schelde estuary.

As the front moved further east, General Dwight Eisenhower faced the dilemma of what route to follow next; in the meantime, his lengthening supply lines were beginning to curtail movement. He preferred to engage the German border at many points, executing a 'broad front policy'. However, Eisenhower acknowledged that the time needed to stockpile ammunition and fuel for such attacks would allow the Germans time to regroup and dig in.

Meanwhile, Field Marshal Bernard Montgomery, 21st Army Group's commander, wanted to push on while the front was still fluid, anxious to deliver a concentrated attack across the Rhine to enter the Ruhr. Montgomery was convinced that a rapid thrust into Germany could end the war before Christmas and within hours of Antwerp falling, he had managed to persuade Eisenhower to try for a knockout blow. In Eisenhower's own words:

> The attractive possibility of quickly turning the German north flank led me to approve the temporary delay in freeing the vital port of Antwerp.

The initial plan, Operation COMET, called upon the 1st Allied Airborne Army to seize bridgeheads over the River Maas at Nijmegen and the River Rhine at Arnhem. However, planning pressures delayed the operation and over the following week the scheme expanded to include ground troops. While three airborne divisions formed a corridor of troops over the rivers, XXX Corps would drive forward crossing the Rhine within forty-eight hours. The new name for expanded scheme was Operation MARKET GARDEN.

Two days before Operation MARKET GARDEN was launched, Eisenhower penned a memorandum to his generals. The Ruhr, Saar and Frankfurt areas were in sight and he wanted a consensus of opinions before deciding future strategy.

Montgomery's reply arrived quickly. He was determined to pursue the narrow front strategy, driving towards the Ruhr.

Although the matter was discussed in detail at Eisenhower's headquarters on 22 September, Montgomery was unable to attend due to the deepening crisis on the road to Arnhem. Instead his Chief of Staff, Major-General Sir Francis de Guingand, heard how the 'possession of an additional major deep water port on our north flank is an indispensable pre-requisite for the final deep drive into Germany'. Everyone present at the meeting agreed that the Allies' future logistical needs were going to be far greater than the present requirements. Without Antwerp, demand would exceed supply. De Guingand returned to his headquarters with new orders for 21st Army Group:

> ...to open the port of Antwerp as a matter of urgency and to develop operations culminating in a strong attack on the Ruhr form the north.

However, Montgomery was first committed to extricating the remnants of the 1st British Airborne Division across the Rhine, followed by a consolidation of his front. Operation MARKET GARDEN had left the right flank of his Army Group holding a

Operations VITALITY and SWITCHBACK cleared the Breskens Pocket and South Beveland

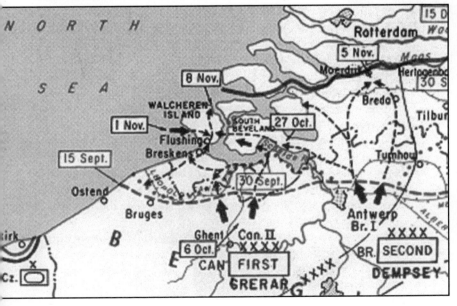

British troops observing Walcheren from Breskens.

precarious salient pointing to Nijmegen.

The 1st Canadian Army received its new directive on 27 September. After clearing Calais and Boulogne, the Canadians were to turn their attentions to the Schelde estuary. Initially, General Simmonds planned to push two divisions north from Antwerp, capturing Bergen-op-Zoom before clearing the South Beveland peninsula. However, before the attack began Montgomery intervened. The Canadians had to create a united front along the south bank of the River Rhine before dealing with the Schelde. Although the advance through Tilburg and 's-Hertogenbosch made strategic sense, it would seriously weaken the forces available to clear the Schelde estuary.

Meetings were held as early as 23 September to discuss the opening of Antwerp and the proposed scheme envisaged three distinct phases. The 2nd Canadian Division would strike north closing South Beveland at Bergen-op-Zoom. The division would then advance west along the peninsula, through the town of Goes as far as Walcheren Island. Meanwhile, the 3rd Canadian Division would clear the small port of Breskens on the south bank of the Schelde. The two operations would be known as VITALITY and SWITCHBACK.

The final stage of the plan, Operation INFATUATE, was

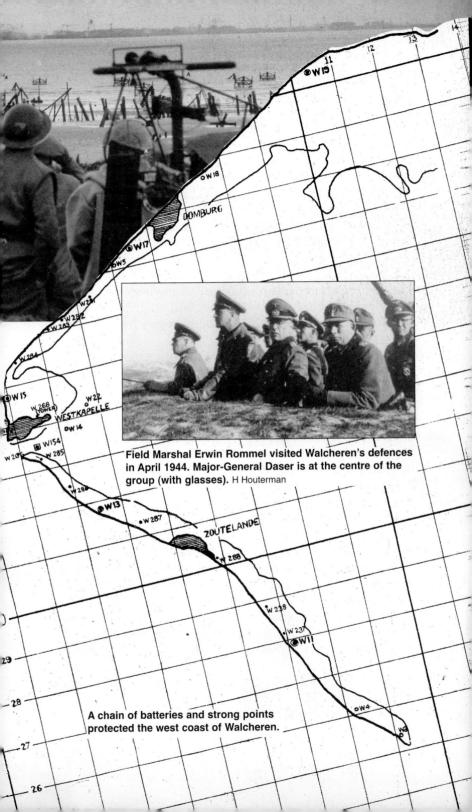

14
13
12
11

W19

W18

DOMBURG

W17

W5

W281

W282

W283

W284

W15

W268 (TOWER)

WESTKAPELLE

W27

W14

W154

W206

W285

Field Marshal Erwin Rommel visited Walcheren's defences in April 1944. Major-General Daser is at the centre of the group (with glasses). H Houterman

W286

W13

W287

ZOUTELANDE

W288

W238

W237

W11

29

28

A chain of batteries and strong points protected the west coast of Walcheren.

27

26

W4

W9

going to be the most dangerous. The First Canadian Army would make an amphibious assault across the Schelde estuary to clear Walcheren Island. The island posed many problems for the Allied planners and the Combined Operation Report compiled after the battle described it as one of the most fortified places in the world. In four years German engineers had built an impressive array of defensive measures, including eighteen major batteries armed with guns of 150mm calibre or above. Many of the guns were fully encased in concrete bunkers and nothing barring a lucky rocket strike could harm the guns or their crews. An impressive array of air defences protected the batteries from air attack.

Offshore hazards were another major concern for the planners. Shoals and sandbanks would make it difficult to sail close to the shore with confidence. Meanwhile, the Germans had littered the estuary with mines and, so far, their coastal batteries had prevented Allied mine sweepers from clearing a safe passage.

A task force also faced a mass of defensive measures on the beaches. Landing craft could be wrecked by an array of concrete blocks, wooden stakes and steel obstacles littering the beaches. Once ashore, the assault troops had to navigate their way through minefields before they could reach the enemy bunkers. Operation INFATUATE was going to be a hazardous undertaking.

CHAPTER TWO

LIFE ON WALCHEREN

The Occupation

Holland finally capitulated in the face of the German Blitzkrieg on 14 May 1940. Walcheren itself had witnessed a fierce battle when two French Territorial Divisions became isolated on the island, trapped by the rapid German advance. Middelburg came under sustained air attack by the Luftwaffe in the fighting that followed and many parts of the old town suffered heavy damage. After the capitulation of the French forces the Zeelanders watched with trepidation as German troops took over their island. It was the start of four and a half years occupation.

As the Dutch looked on grimly, it soon became clear that the Germans were intent on defending their island at all costs. While the Germans continued to advance across Europe, Africa and Russia the Zeelanders were resigned to the fact that the Third Reich would indeed last for a thousand years. Liberation was an impossible dream and at first co-operation was a steady source of income. There was plenty of work for the willing and

The local population had to quickly adapt to the occupation

88mm anti aircraft guns situated on the coastline of Walcheren where they could be used against shipping and in defence of the island against invasion.

German 155mm gun. Coastal batteries guarded against a seabourne invasion

some worked on the huge coastal batteries along the dunes. Before long a network of bunkers began to spring up, creating mini-fortresses all over the island. Although food was scarce, many fields had to be left fallow as the Germans laid large minefields to protect their defensive positions.

Life was hard and many were forced to hand over their homes to the German garrison troops, while they themselves slept in barns. As the war dragged on food and clothing became scarce. Even so the Zeelanders considered themselves fortunate compared with their countrymen in the north. The island is a rich arable area and many were able to supplement their diets with locally grown food.

For the first two years life carried on virtually unchanged for the majority of Zeelanders. However, with the defeat of the German Armies in 1942, first in Russia and then Africa, the Dutch realised that their occupiers were not invincible. Although dreams of liberation now looked as though they could become reality, it was still a long way off. Meanwhile, the terms of German occupation grew harsher as the fortunes of war turned against them. Zeeland is a strong Protestant area and as the months passed few noticed the discreet round up of the small Jewish community. No one knew or dared to ask where their absent neighbours had gone and the only reminder is the memorial in Middelburg's Jewish Cemetery.

As the war began to turn against the Germans, they took steps to censor news about the war. The official Dutch press was under strict German control and many eagerly read the underground newspapers distributed occasionally by intrepid journalists. Although illegal newsletters kept morale high, they were often made at a terrible price. One hundred and twenty Dutch Underground members were executed after the Germans infiltrated the largest paper, the *Trouw*, the *Faithful*. The next stage of censorship came in 1943 when personal radio sets were confiscated.

Even so, news reached the local population via hidden radio sets, and in June 1944 the islanders were heartened to hear that the Allies had landed in Normandy. Throughout the summer, as the German armies fell back across the Low Countries, the Zeelanders waited eagerly for their turn to be liberated. As the Allied spearheads reached the Schelde at the beginning of September it appeared that the German Army had been defeated. The fall of Antwerp sealed off the south bank of the great river and the Dutch watched eagerly as a host of craft ferried defeated troops from Breskens. Although many of the retreating troops passed through Walcheren heading for the mainland, the island's garrison continued working to perfect their fortifications. As fighting began in earnest in the Breskens pocket, only a few miles away across the estuary, the Dutch sensed that the Germans intended to defend every inch of their island.

With the front line so close, food became scarce and life became unbearable when electricity supplies failed. The cold and hungry islanders despaired as they waited for their liberation, however, Walcheren was not on the immediate list of objectives for the Allied Command.

The Germans

As the Allies planned to attack Walcheren Island, 8,000 German troops prepared to defend the fortress they had created. The backbone of the defence was the 70th Infantry Division,

Thousands of troops manned Walcheren's coastal defences.

commanded by *Generalleutnant* Wilhelm Daser. Many of its soldiers were suffering from dyspeptic disorders or stomach complaints. To combat their eating ailments, each unit had a special bakery to make white bread, a luxury throughout the German forces. Despite the derogatory nickname given to the division, *Das Brotweiss*, (The White Bread Division) some of the troops were hardened veterans of the Russian front, others were garrison troops, men in their thirties and forties who had never seen action. The mixture of experience and fanaticism of the men was something that the commandos would have to come to terms with as they fought their way across the island. Each party

General Daser, prior to taking command of the 70th Division. H Houterman

of men acted differently, according to their ultimate objective and in many cases their leadership. Some surrendered at the first opportunity while others would fight to the end.

The two battalions of the 1019th Grenadier Regiment, under *Oberst* Eugen Reinhardt, were stationed on the south part of the island. While the 1st Battalion held Flushing town, the 2nd Battalion was responsible for the south-east area of the island, from Fort Rammekens to the Sloedam. The division's second

Oberst Rienhardt (left) checks the floodwater level in Flushing. H Houterman

Seekommandant, Kapitän zur See Frank Aschmann.
H Houterman

regiment, the 1020th Grenadier Regiment, was stationed on the north-west part of the island, covering Westkapelle, Domburg and Oostkapelle. The Division's fusilier and pioneer battalions were responsible for the east side of the island.

Naval troops guarded the coast under the leadership of *Seekommandant, Kapitän zur See* Frank Aschmann. His organisation was split into two distinct areas of responsibility. *Marine Artillerie Abteilung* 202, led by *Korvettenkapitän* Robert Opalka, manned the formidable coastal batteries, including W19 at Oostkapelle, W17 at Domburg, W15 at Westkapelle, W13 at Zoutelande and W11 at Dishoek. The air defence was controlled by Flak Abteilung 810, commanded by *Korvettenkapitän* Hans Köll. Although they had been positioned to engage enemy aircraft, many of the flak cannons were equally capable of engaging offshore or ground targets. In many cases the marines would prove to be fanatical opponents prepared to fight from their bunkers until the last moment.

Finally, *Festungsstormmtruppen* (Fortress Base Troops) manned a chain of pillboxes and observation posts covering the dunes between the coastal batteries. These garrison troops were often middle-aged family men with dubious fighting qualities.

Keeping watch over the Scheldt estuary.

Chapter Three

PLANNING OPERATION INFATUATE

Bombing the Island

All levels of command agreed that Walcheren was a formidable position and, after an attack by airborne troops had been ruled out First Canadian Army looked to Bomber Command to soften up the German garrison. Previous experience has shown that prolonged bombing 'would not constitute an effective and economical employment of our bomber effort'; at this stage in the war there were far more tempting targets across Germany. The plan was to strike the island with every available plane during the forty-eight hours prior to D-Day.

Meanwhile, the Army wanted to know if it would be possible to breach the dikes. Large parts of Walcheren Island were below high water level and by creating gaps in the dikes sea water would flood substantial parts of the island. The chance to paralyse the German command and control was a tempting proposition. While many of the inshore bunkers would be uninhabitable, the batteries on the coastal dunes would be cut off from supplies.

Despite the military advantages, breaching the dikes created a moral problem. Heavy bombing would inevitably lead to civilian casualties, the flooding would bring misery for the local population, causing extensive damage to property. The inrush of salt water would lead to contamination of the fertile land, possibly depriving the local population of a livelihood for years to come.

Despite the drawbacks, Allied command was firmly fixed on the overall war objectives and on 29 September Bomber Command agreed to attack the dike south of Westkapelle, at the thinnest part of the sea wall. The date was set for 3 October, the next spring tide. Although the Dutch government knew that Walcheren was a target, the true nature of the raid was never revealed on the grounds that they would object strongly. The deception would lead to a greater loss of life.

As the RAF prepared to strike, attempts were made to warn

Lancasters of RAF Bomber Command on a daylight bombing mission in 1944. *Right*: The results of the bombing on Westkapelle – the dike walls were breached allowing the sea to rush in. The town was devastated by fire and water.

the local population. On 2 October hundreds of warning leaflets were scattered across the island, while messages were broadcast on the BBC Home Service. Bomber formations often passed over Walcheren but on this occasion it was imperative that the people knew they were in the target zone. The following morning 247 bombers from No 8 (Pathfinder Force) Group RAF and No 1, 3 and 5 (Bomber) Groups RAF crossed the North Sea heading for Westkapelle. Bomber command had never attempted an operation such as this before, and was not entirely convinced that it was possible to cut the dike. It was after all over seventy metres wide at the base, tapering to twenty metres at the apex. Just before 1:00pm, the first wave of thirty bombers began releasing their cargo, composed of 1,000lb and 4,000lb bombs. Anti-aircraft fire was non-existent and by the time the final wave passed over the village, sea water was starting to spread across the island. The breach was initially estimated at thirty-five metres wide, but the inrush of water, quickly doubled the size of the gap.

Civilian casualties in Westkapelle had been heavy. Over 150 lost their lives, a terrible blow to the small community. Several families had gathered in the basement of the local windmill, *De*

Seawater quickly spread across the island following the first bombing raid. IWM C4676

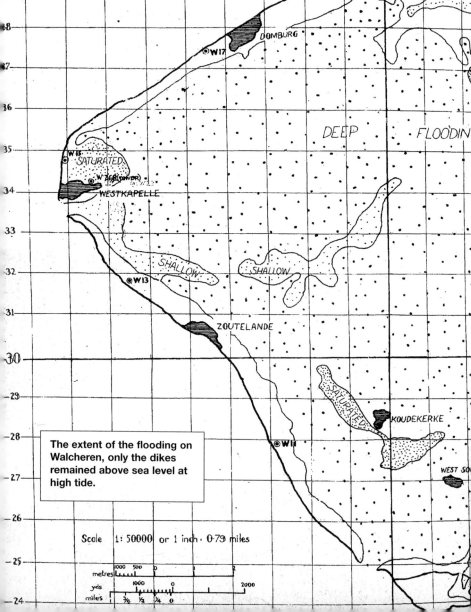

WESTKAPELLE GAP

DOMBURG

DEEP FLOODIN

SATURATED

WESTKAPELLE

SHALLOW SHALLOW

ZOUTELANDE

SATURATED

KOUDEKERKE

WEST SO

The extent of the flooding on Walcheren, only the dikes remained above sea level at high tide.

Scale 1:50000 or 1 inch · 0·79 miles

metres 1000 500 0 1 2

yds 1000 0 2000

miles 3/4 1/2 1/4 0

Roos Molen (Rose Mill) owned by the Theune family. A stray bomb damaged the mill, trapping forty-seven men, women and children inside. Although many survived the blast, the encroaching sea water flooded the shelter, drowning all but three of the occupants.

Aerial reconnaissance noted that at high tide, sea water covered large parts of the island, flooding many houses to a depth of a metre. Twice a day the people of Walcheren had to watch helplessly as their homes slowly filled with salt water and stinking mud.

Now that all parties knew it was possible to cut the dike, 21 Army Group requested more raids to complete the 'sinking' of the island. On 7 October, raids either side of Flushing created two breaches, effectively flooding the southern half of the island. Over 350 tonnes of bombs, delivered by fifty-eight Lancasters and Mosquitos, tore a hole in the dike west of the town. Meanwhile, sixty-four bombers cut the sea wall east of the town docks. Four days later No 5 (Bomber) Group completed the flooding, cutting the dike on the north side of the island, near Veere.

Over the following weeks, over 5,000 tonnes of high explosive rained down on the coastal batteries. Although there

Bomber command tried in vain to destroy Walcheren's coastal batteries.
IWM CL1482

was no doubt that it needed a 'lucky hit' to immobilise a gun, they could not be allowed to hamper minesweeping operations unmolested.

As planning proceeded, there were concerns that the Westkapelle coastal batteries could decimate the landing. If the bulk of the landing force could pass through the gap, they could disembark in the dead ground behind the dike. Widening the gap could mean the difference between success and failure. A request to Bomber Command resulted in 106 Squadron (Lancasters) delivering over one hundred 1,000lb bombs on 17 October. The raid accomplished its objective, nearly doubling the size of the gap. Over the next two weeks the tides carved a smooth channel wide enough for landing craft to pass through.

The stage was now set for the assault. Two huge raids, comprising over 500 aircraft, showered the island with nearly 3,000 tonnes of explosives on the 28th and 29th. However, a request to Bomber Command, asking for a last minute raid on the coastal defences protecting Flushing, was denied. Pinpoint bombing in darkness was impossible and it was likely that the town would be devastated by such a strike. The assault on Flushing would have to depend on the artillery of 2nd Canadian Corps massing on the southern shore of the estuary for support.

Operation DETACHED

Before First Canadian Army could begin to prepare an invasion plan, it needed accurate information to locate a suitable landing area. Some details had been gathered from refugees and aerial photographs, but following the lessons learnt in Normandy, steps were being taken to study the beaches at first hand. This dangerous task fell on the shoulders of special men. Landing parties, known by the somewhat derogatory code word of 'Tarbrush', would silently approach the beaches under the cover of darkness and, if possible, land. Once ashore, they could assess the state of the beach defences as well as the suitability of the shoreline.

The plan was to establish two beachheads on the same day, one in the region of Flushing with the second near Westkapelle. With the help of local information, 'Keepforce', under the command of Captain Raymond Keep, managed to assess the shoreline of Flushing. After a detailed study of the shoreline, a small disused harbour, known as the Ooster of Dockhaven, was chosen for the landing. Although it could only accommodate two landing craft at a time, the beach provided adequate shelter from the town's defences.

The landing at Westkapelle posed a completely different set of problems. The plan was to sail a large part of the landing force through the gap in the dike, in the hope of avoiding the coastal batteries in the area. However, the planners needed an accurate assessment of the area before they could confidently plan the operation.

The first attempt was made on the night of 15 October, but as Lieutenant-Commander J Whitby's MTB drifted towards Westkapelle alert sentries opened fire and he had to escape at full power. Two night later the 'Tarbrush' party transferred to their Dory (a small powered launch able to land on the beach), and managed to drift up to the beach before they were seen. Yet again Keep's men managed to extricate themselves under heavy fire. A third attempt to study the beach on the night of the 27th was rather more successful. This time Whitby's men went unnoticed and they managed to make notes on the layout of the beach obstacles as the Dory drifted silently along the coastline.

From the information gleaned, the planners could make a decision on zero hour; and the options were extremely limited. The landing could not take place around low tide due to off shore sandbanks. Meanwhile, 'Tarbrush' had noted that inrush of water through the gap at high tide could capsize the commandos' amphibious vehicles. The landing would have to take place at half tide and the engineers needed time to clear the beach obstacles before they were covered by the incoming tide. Brigadier Bernard Leicester estimated his men would need five

Rows of obstacles lined the beaches of Walcheren.   **A 'Hedgehog'**

A German casemate equipped with a captured Soviet field gun.

hours of daylight to establish a beachhead. The combination of factors only left one small window of opportunity any delay and the rising tide would jeopardise the landing.

The Germans had spent four years preparing the beaches against an invasion and once ashore, the commandos faced a formidable array of defences. Concrete blocks had been dragged out along the beach below the high water mark and contact mines, capable of ripping through the skin of a landing craft, were set on top of each block. A line of 'Hedgehogs', steel obstacles capable of snagging a passing craft, had been set just below the high water mark. Rows of sturdy stakes ran parallel to the surf and some had been booby-trapped with shells drilled into the top. Belts of coiled barbed wire protected the top of the dike and there were extra perimeter fences protecting the defensive positions. The seaward dunes had also been mined with a mixture of anti-tank and anti-personnel mines. The final obstacle, a triple row of steel rails cast into a concrete beam, had to be crossed before the commandos could leave the beach.

Brigadier Leicester's men faced new perils as they tried to make headway inland. Aerial photographs pinpointed

Brigadier Leicester.

comprehensive defensive positions in the vicinity of the gap. Eight pillboxes protected the inland side of the dikes and extensive entrenchments had been carved into the bomb craters either side of the gap in the dike.

A few days before the assault Brigadier Leicester was told that the promised armoured support was to be withdrawn, on the grounds that the island was flooded most of the time. Leicester was furious; the suggestion would leave his men dependent on their own heavy weapons once they crossed the dike. Eventually sense prevailed after a series of objections from Leicester, the commandos' precious armoured support was reinstated.

As October grew to a close, the assault force began to assemble and while 155 Brigade gathered around Breskens, 4 Special Service Brigade trained on the dunes near Ostend. In turn, the men trained with landing craft and learnt how to co-operate with armour. They also had to come to terms with the new amphibious vehicles, the Buffalo and the Weasel. They would prove to be the only reliable form of transport on the flooded island.

Preliminary Bombardments

Great emphasis had been placed on suppressing the coastal batteries during the landing at Westkapelle. Although many inland sites had been made uninhabitable by the flooding, there were still five active batteries on the coastline. W17, armed with four 220mm guns, and W19, complete with four 105mm pieces covered the northern coast of the island. Meanwhile, the four 150mm guns of W15 overlooked the north side of the gap. W13, situated half way between Westkapelle and Zoutelande, could fire along the coast with its battery of four 150mm guns. W11, further along the coast at Dishoek, could also shell the landing beaches.

The plan was to engage the batteries from a variety of sources. The fire plan would open at H-70, beginning with an artillery barrage by 9th Army Group Royal Artillery and 2nd Canadian Group Royal Artillery. The two Army Groups were based on the south side of the estuary, several miles from their targets. More than ninety heavy and super-heavy guns would target the batteries. Three warships would accompany the task force to target the coastal batteries. (A bombing schedule was also prepared but poor weather would prevent Bomber Command from taking part.)

· At H-50 fighter-bombers of 84 Group RAF would strafe the weapon pits and trenches either side of the gap with their rockets and bombs. Meanwhile, Boston aircraft would fly overhead craft laying smoke screens to shield the landing craft.

THE LANDING PLANS

INFATUATE I – The Landing at Flushing

Major-General Edmund Hakewill Smith, commanding officer of 52nd (Lowland) Division, had overall responsibility for the

Major-General Hakewill-Smith

assault on the island. Although 155 Brigade, under Brigadier James McLaren, was given the task of clearing Flushing, No 4 Commando (men specially trained for amphibious assaults) had been attached to the Brigade to lead the assault. 'Keepforce's' men at 5:45am would lead the way in, marking the approach and clearing a path off the beach. The first wave of 4 Commando would land soon after, securing the immediate area around the beach. The troops that followed would head into the heart of the town as quickly as possible, and it was hoped that Lieutenant-Colonel Christian Melville's men would be able to establish a perimeter by dawn. Two French Troops from 10 (Inter-Allied) Commando had been added to 4 Commando for the attack. The squadron of LCAs, under Lieutenant-Commander Stuart Vernon RNVR, would return to Breskens harbour to begin ferrying the three battalions of 155 Brigade across the estuary. 4th King's Own Scottish Borderers would land first, followed by the 5th King's Own Scottish Borderers and 7/9th Royal Scots.

INFATUATE II - The Landing at Westkapelle

Brigadier-General McLaren

Special troops were required to carry out the landing at Westkapelle and Simmonds was offered the services of Brigadier Bernard 'Jumbo' Leicester's 4th Special Service Brigade. The commandos were veterans of many amphibious assaults, spear-heading the British landings in Normandy. This, however, was going to be one of their toughest tests so far and one, which all who survived, would never forget.

Brigadier Leicester was pleased to discover that Captain Anthony Pugsley DSO RN would be leading the naval side of the operation. The two officers had successfully worked together on Normandy only a few months before. The task force, code named 'T Force', included 130 ships of all shapes and sizes; ranging from a battleship armed with fifteen-inch guns down to small motor launches.

Captain Pugsley and Commander Sellar.

Captain Marcel Kelsey RN led the Bombardment Squadron, comprising three capital ships: the battleship HMS *Warspite* and the Monitors HMS *Roberts* and HMS *Erebus*. With the aid of spotter aircraft, *Warspite* would bombard the batteries either side of Domburg to the north during the landings, while *Roberts* shelled targets south of the landing beaches. Meanwhile, *Erebus* would shell Westkapelle Battery, to the north of the village.

Ostend docks began to fill with a variety of vessels as D-Day drew close. As well as the landing craft designated to carry 4 Special Service Brigade, there were the support craft designed to provide direct fire support during the final 'run-in' to the beach. Landing craft were large and cumbersome, with a maximum speed of only a few knots. Hard lessons learnt in the Mediterranean and off the coast of Normandy had shown that air support and naval support was inadequate and at times unsafe. Observers noticed that shore gunners instinctively targeted any craft firing on them and naval planners had designed a variety of craft to exploit this human trait. The Support Squadron 'Eastern Flank' led by Captain Kenneth 'Monkey' Sellar DSC, RN would provide close support during the final approach to the beach.

The larger support craft were converted LCT (Landing Craft Tank) Mark IV, a craft originally designed to carry up to twelve vehicles. By welding the loading ramp shut and adding decking, the craft became a floating platform for a variety of

The 'Buffalo' was able to transport men across land and water.

The smaller 'Weasel' often struggled to cope the difficult conditions on Walcheren. H Houterman

weapons. However, with a maximum speed of ten knots and measuring seventy metres long, the support craft were ideal targets.

As the Task Force approached the shore, the Support Squadron swung into action, drawing fire from the landing craft carrying the commandos. The first craft to engage the beach were the LCT (R) (Landing Craft Tank – Rockets). Six hundred rocket tubes, each one firing a projectile equal to a six-inch shell, covered the decking of the ship. A rocket strike could shower the beach with missiles; destroying soft targets and detonating mines. The crew of the LCG (M)s (Landing Craft Gun – Medium) in the taskforce had one of the most dangerous tasks. The craft would beach opposite their targets to provide a stable firing platform for the turret-mounted 17-pounder guns. Meanwhile, the LCG (Landing Craft Gun) would sail close to the shoreline to engage pillboxes with their two 4.7" guns. LCS (L) (Landing Craft Support – Light) small vulnerable craft armed with 6-pounder guns and machine-guns, would fire at targets on the beach in the hope of drawing fire from the rest of the task force. LCF (Landing Craft Flak) were initially devised to provide cover from air attack but since the Allies achieved air superiority, the craft had been used as a close support weapon. Their two pounder pom-poms and Oerlikon cannons would add to the overall effect of the close support fire.

While Captain Sellars' support craft fought an unequal battle with the shore batteries, the assault troops would sail ashore in N Squadron's LCTs, led by Lieutenant-Commander Bernard Arbuthnot RN. Although the first wave of commandos would go ashore in LCI (S) (Landing Craft Infantry – Small), the rest of 4 Special Service Brigade would land in LCTs complete with their amphibious vehicles. It was hoped that the commandos' Buffaloes, each one capable of carrying thirty men, would be able to drive ashore. Smaller vehicles, known as Weasels, would carry their supplies and heavy equipment.

Four LCTs, each carrying an armoured assault team, would beach alongside the first wave. Specialist tanks, nicknamed 'Funnies', were designed to overcome the array of beach obstacles. Sherman flail tanks, manned by the 1st Lothians, were armed with a huge drum covered in a series of ball and chains. As the tank crawled forward the drum rotated at high speed, beating a way through the minefields on the beach. Churchill

Flail tank for clearing minefields.

Facine carrier for filling holes etc.

Petard tank for destroying strongpoints.

Bobbin tank for putting a track across soft ground.

AVRE tanks, provided by 87th Assault Squadron Royal Engineers, were armed with 90mm Petard guns. They could blast a way through obstacles on the beach before moving on to deal with pillboxes. 'Bobbin Tanks' carried rolled mats which could be laid across soft sand or mud, letting other vehicles follow on behind.

Once they were off the beach, the tanks faced a steep drop at the far side of the dike. Working together, tanks armed with fascines (huge bundles of wood that could be dropped into ditches or craters) and bridge tanks, could build a roadway down into the village. A number of bulldozers completed the assault teams and they would be called on to perform a variety of tasks; ranging from clearing obstacles, filling craters and levelling roads. Once the beachhead was secure, the bulldozers would create a cutting through the dunes complete with storage bays and slit trenches. Each team possessed three flails, two AVRE's and a D7 Bulldozer.

The landing area at Westkapelle was split into three beaches – Tare Red, Tare White and Tare Green. The first wave, comprising three troops of 41 Royal Marine Commando, would land on Tare Red at H–5 and seize the top of the dike overlooking the village. Four LCT (Landing Craft Tank) carrying the armoured assault teams would disembark alongside the commandos.

At H + 5, LCTs would nose through the gap beaching behind the dike. Two troops from 41 Royal Marine Commando would land on the north side of the gap, entering Westkapelle under covering fire from their comrades on the dike. Meanwhile, the leading troops of 48 Royal Marine Commando would land on the south side of the gap and head towards the pillboxes and radar station covering the beach. A third wave of craft would land the remainder of 41 and 48 Royal Marine Commandos at H + 25. The next wave would bring 47 Royal Marine Commando ashore at H + 60. Two LCTs would bring the 4 Special Service Brigade's tactical headquarters ashore at the same time.

Tare Green was 800 metres south of the gap and as soon as the dunes had been cleared, landing craft could start to bring vital stores ashore.

Men of the 52 (Lowland) Infantry Division on their landing craft prior to Operation INFATUATE.

CHAPTER FOUR

INFATUATE I – ASSAULT ON FLUSHING

At 2:00am on 1 November, the men of 4 Commando were roused from their billets in the ruins of Breskens. The cold drizzle did little to lift the soldiers' spirits as they made their way down to the embarkation point. Shells from over three hundred guns screamed overhead towards Flushing and showers of sparks lit up the horizon as they found their target. Mosquitoe fighter-bombers flew low overhead to strafe targets across the estuary. However, low cloud meant that the high level bombing had already been cancelled. The men quietly took their places in the LCAs without interruption and at 4:40am the first pair of landing craft slipped their moorings and headed for Flushing.

Fires cast an eerie glow across the horizon as the landing craft approached the shore and the flames illuminated the windmill to the left of Uncle beach; there would be no mistake about where to land. 'Keepforce', the men who had surveyed the beach a few days earlier, guided 4 Commando LCAs ashore.

LCAs crowd Breskens harbour

LCAs ferry troops across the Schelde estuary while Flushing burns on the horizon. H Houterman

LCAs prepare to land on Uncle Beach. H Houterman

Two of 'Keepforce's patrol craft led the way in, followed by a section of 1 Troop under Captain Dennis Rewcastle. Although the craft approached the shore unseen, one of the patrol boats swung starboard, away from the beach, in the darkness. Disaster was averted at the last moment when the second patrol boat found the correct landing point, beaching on the end of the Orange Mill promontory. As the beach clearing party set about cutting wire and laying tape across Uncle Beach, their commander, Lieutenant Harry Hargreaves DSC, RNVR, set up a guiding lamp at the end of the promontory ready to guide the next wave ashore.

While 'Keepforce's men prepared the shoreline, Rewcastle's troop set about securing the beachhead. Moving quickly, they clambered onto the sea wall, taking a number of prisoners along the way. CSM Lewis' group burst into a strong point near the Orange Mill, finding twenty Germans cowering on the floor inside. They were the crew of a 75mm gun. Rewscastle's men also captured the crew of the beach searchlight in an underground shelter at the shore end of the promontory. Leaving a patrol to block the entrance to Oranjestraat, Captain Rewcastle's men began to clear the block of streets to the north of Oranjemolen, an area code named 'Seaford'. They were well on their way to securing the western approach to the beach.

Meanwhile, Lieutenant John Hunter-Grey's section, from No 2 Troop, headed east to tackle a number of strong points along the shoreline. Sergeant Stanley Mullard's men burst into the first pillbox, finding twenty startled Germans and a 50mm anti-tank gun.

While the advanced parties cleared the perimeter of the beachhead 'Keepforce' guided the next two LCA's in, carrying the rest of No 1 Troop and No 2 Troop. Lieutenant Peter King's section, landed unopposed, and headed along Oranjestraat towards the Willelm III Barracks. Finding it empty, they headed west along the seafront to engage two machine-guns firing on the approaching landing craft. The commandos quickly overpowered the crews, bringing in ten prisoners. As King's men headed towards the Arsenal, another machine-gun post came to life on the promontory code named 'Brighton', firing across the face of the old harbour. While half the section returned fire, the remainder of King's men joined No 1 Troop in 'Seaford'.

Meanwhile, Lieutenant Frank Albrow's section, from No 2 Troop, had landed unscathed and taken up fire positions covering Lieutenant Hunter-Gray's advance along the shore line. No 2 Troop advanced quickly through the area code named 'Troon', clearing seven defensive positions before the Germans realised what was happening. Mullard's captured anti-tank gun played an active part in the advance after his men wheeled it out of its gun pit. A German 75mm gun was also pressed into action, engaging targets on the opposite side of the dock. The scratch crew quickly developed the necessary skills to fire their new weapon, silencing two machine-guns and a flak gun. With the area code named 'Troon' clear, Lieutenant Albrow moved his men forward sealing off the promontory code named 'Falmouth'.

So far the landing was progressing well and the first wave of troops had established a small beachhead. Captain Alastair Thorburn's Troop had sealed off the town approach while Captain 'Jack' Wilson's men had secured the area east of the beach. Many Germans were caught off guard, surrendering to

Uncle Beach and the Harbour; the arrows chart No 3 Troop's route into the heart of the town.

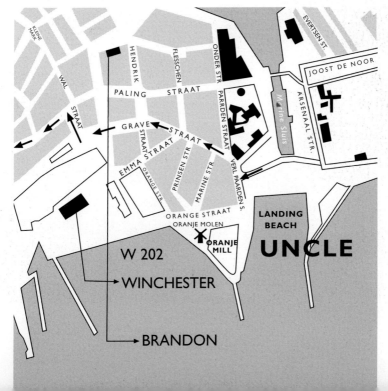

the commandos at the first opportunity.

While the leading troops secured the flanks of Uncle beach, No 3 Troop prepared to land. As Major Gordon Webb's men braced themselves for the landing, a 20mm flak cannon opened fire. It was, however, firing blindly and as the commandos stepped ashore, they watched anxiously as tracer streaked overhead.

After assembling beyond the dike, Webb's men headed towards their first objective, Bellamypark (code name 'Braemar'), in the centre of the town. Moving quickly along Gravestraat, No 3 Troop made their way to Wilhelminastraat. Finding the old harbour under fire from the pillbox code-named 'Brighton', Webb diverted his men along Nieuwstraat. Although the occasional sniper or machine-gun opened fire on the troops as they ran along the dark streets, No 3 Troop only suffered one casualty.

No 2 Section came across a pillbox as they entered Bellamypark and while Sergeant Jackson led an assault on the

strong point, the rest of the section fanned out around the park. The pillbox only managed to fire a few rounds, killing Private Pierre Laux, but its capture made it possible to begin clearing the houses around the park. Although resistance was light, Lieutenant Nicholas Barrass was killed during the house clearing.

While No 2 Section cleared Bellamypark, No 1 Section, under Captain Murdoch McDougall, took the lead. Intelligence had reported that the Germans had established a naval barracks along the sea front. Huge pillboxes dominated Boulevard de Ruyter, so McDougall's men were going to enter through the maze of streets behind the barracks.

It was now beginning to get light and as time passed, the Germans were beginning to realise that they were being attacked. The section pressed on, stumbling on a startled group of Germans at one corner. In the fire-fight that followed the commandos caused ten casualties for the loss of one of their own. Captain McDougall quickly ordered his men off the street;

Taking cover as shells target the landing beach.

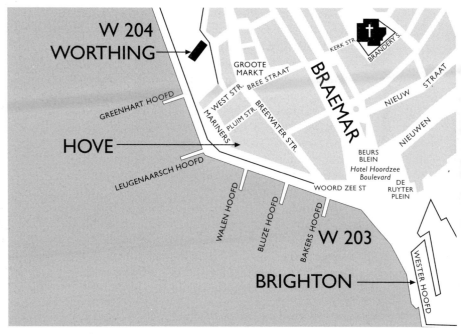

The area surrounding Bellamy Park, 4 Commando encountered resistance from 'Brighton', 'Hove' and 'Worthing'.

French Commandos pose for a moment at the Orange Mill.
H Houterman

Commandos cross Bellamy Park under fire.

now that the Germans were aroused, snipers and machine-guns would soon cover every street. Anxious to keep moving, McDougall's men advanced by any possible means, climbing over sheds and garden walls to reach 'Hove'. However, 'Brighton' pillbox, overlooking the harbour, still continued to harass No 1 Section. Captain McDougall was forced to post sentries in the houses along the line of his advance, in case the Germans decided to counter-attack.

Although his position was secure for the time being, McDougall had insufficient men to clear the naval barracks. A few men were sent into the complex, and by working their way through the maze of rooms established a number of lookout posts covering many of the exits. By the time it was light, McDougall's commandos were severely limiting the Germans' movements throughout the barracks.

Although No 3 Troop had managed to clear a large part of its objectives, it was in danger of being over stretched. Major Webb requested reinforcements, but difficulties elsewhere in the town would leave him disappointed; his men would have to hold their positions until nightfall.

Meanwhile, back at the beach, the Germans had started to target the landing area and the two LCA's carrying No 5 Troop came under intense fire as they made their final run-in. The first LCA was hit in the engine compartment, wounding the coxswain. The out of control landing craft soon rammed into the pier, sinking as the commandos disembarked under heavy machine-gun fire. Heavy fire struck the second craft as it approached the beach. In the confusion, Captain Alexandre Lofi's men disembarked too early, plunging into shoulder deep water.

After wading onto the beach, Lieutenants Paul Chaussé and Pierre Amaury cursed their bad luck as they assembled their men. The troop followed a similar route to No 3 Troop, making its way along Oranjestraat, Emmastraat and Wilheminastraat. Chaussé's section came under fire as they entered Gravestraat, but after few rounds from the section's 2-inch mortar the enemy

post was quickly overrun. Next came St Jacob's Church in the Oude Markt, where a solitary prisoner was taken.

No 2 Section moved quickly along Kerkstraat and across Bellamypark, heading down Breestraat. The plan was for Lieutenant Amaury to take up a defensive position in the Groote Markt while Lieutenant Chaussé attacked the barracks along the sea front. Heavy machine-gun and sniper fire greeted Amaury's section as it entered the market place and after taking cover in the houses and shops, the commandos began working their way around the square. In the face of such opposition, the Germans withdrew into their barracks on the sea front, codenamed 'Worthing'.

While his men prepared for the assault, Lieutenant Chaussé crept forward to find the safest approach route. He was met

It became almost impossible to move after first light as German snipers and machine guns came alive. WM BU1245

with a shower of stick grenades and, as Sergeants Paillet and Messanot dragged their wounded officer to safety, it was clear that the way forward was blocked. For the time being, No 5 Troop would have to consolidate its position around Groote Markt and await reinforcements.

No 6 Troop, under Captain Guy Vourch, had the furthest to travel to reach their objective. At the north end of the old town, between the inland lake known as Binnenbozem and the shipbuilding yards was a major crossroads, code named 'Bexhill'. Any German reinforcements intent on reaching the centre of the town had to pass the junction and Vourch's task was to seize the area as quickly as possible. The machine-gun section would accompany the Troop, consolidating the crossroads position after it had been taken.

Although machine-gun fire strafed the Troop's LCAs as they hit the beach, casualties were light. Vourch was unable to locate the machine-gun section as his men assembled behind the dike and with strict instructions to move as quickly as possible, No 6 Troop set off alone.

The Troop's first objective, the Post office in Steenen Beer, was strongly held. Most of the occupants, however, relented in the face of a charge delivered by Lieutenant Jacques Senée's section. A grenade dealt with a handful that refused to surrender. Continuing through the town along Walstraat, Vourch's men were hailed by many civilians awaked by the noise of battle. A Dutch section accompanied Vourch's men, liasing with the local population en route. The section leader, Hendrik van Nahüys, a former Flushing police officer, used his local knowledge to make good progress.

The troop reached 'Bexhill' at 7:45 and the lead section, followed by Vourch's headquarters crossed Coosje Buskenstraat to take up positions covering the junction. 'Dover' pillbox, on the sea front, opened fire as the commandos dashed across the road. The strong point possessed a 20mm flak gun, a devastating weapon at short range. The street was under careful watch by the time the second section arrived. For the time being, No 6 Troop was spilt in two. Before Captain Vourch had time to take stock of his position, he faced two problems. One sub-section entered a school overlooking the crossroads, taking seven prisoners. The large building was quickly turned into a defensive position, securing the commandos grip on the crossroads. Meanwhile, lookouts spotted a large group of Germans, about a company strong, moving down Badhuisstraat towards the crossroads. Setting up a hasty fire position the commandos opened fire, scattering the hostile reinforcements. Captain Vourch had arrived just in time; minutes later and 'Bexhill' would have been in German hands.

Although Vourch held the junction, his Troop was split in two halves. To make matters worse, at a time when every man was needed, Nahüys had mistakenly led one sub-section west towards the sea front. Infiltrating Germans managed to cut the group off, and many did not return until the following day. Lieutenant Guy de Montlaur's attempt to enter the shipyard gates east of the crossroads was thwarted by a machine-gun post along Aagje Dekenstraat. As his men did their best to form a tight defensive perimeter, Captain Vourch wondered where the lost machine-gun section was.

Two pillboxes opened fire as No 4 Troop, the support weapons troop, approached the beach in two LCAs. Although the Bren gun on Captain Knyveth Carr's LCA returned fire, it made little difference and bullets raked the LCAs on the run in to the beach. Just before it hit the shore the craft struck an iron

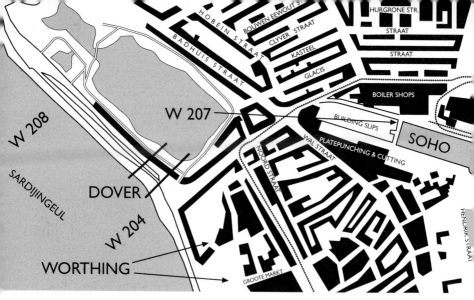

The bottlenecks at Bexhill and Dover threatened to stifle 4 Commando's advance.

bar, bringing it to a shuddering halt. Clambering into the water, Carr's men did their best to salvage their equipment under heavy machine-gun fire. Meanwhile, the LCA carrying the medium machine-gun section landed safely alongside.

As the troop assembled under cover of the sea wall, Captain Carr returned to the stricken craft and with the help of Staff-Sergeant Lloyd and Private Leyland, retrieved a second mortar and several cases of bombs. Within half an hour, the mortars were cleaned, in position and ready to fire.

The machine-gun section set off in search of No 6 troop and eventually reached 'Bexhill' fifteen minutes late. Lieutenant C A Kelly ran across the junction under fire, making contact with Captain Vourch. On the return journey, a sniper found his mark hitting Kelly in the chest. His batman managed to drag the wounded officer into a nearby shop. The first crew was about to cross when the same sniper hit Lance-Corporal Lambert in the stomach. As Private John Stoddart ran out to recover Lambert's tripod, another shot rang out, leaving Stoddart mortally wounded, shot in the head. Captain Carr could see that the crossroads was too dangerous a place, and led the rest of the section along Scherminkelstraat, to find a safer place to cross. Under cover of smoke and supporting fire from one of the section's Bren guns, Carr managed to get the rest of his men across safely.

By 8:30am No 4 Commando had established a tight perimeter in Flushing old town. Through moving quickly, and ignoring isolated groups of Germans, the commandos now held key positions. No 3 Troop and No 5 Troop had established a defensive line in the west of the town, behind the seafront, while No 6 Troop held 'Bexhill' junction with assistance from the support troop. While No 2 Troop had sealed off the eastern side of the beachhead, No 1 Troop had assembled in reserve awaiting further orders.

Lieutenant-Colonel Dawson.

Knowing that help was on its way, Lieutenant-Colonel Robert Dawson was anxious to locate his forward line so he could make further plans. So far radio contact had not been established with the three companies in the north or west of the town and Melville had to rely on runners. Lieutenant Hattu braved sniper fire to locate No 3 and No 5 Troops, reporting that both Troops faced heavy resistance. Although 4 Commando had the situation under control for the time being, reinforcements would be needed before they could make further progress.

4th King's Own Scottish Borderers

Twenty-six LCAs, carrying the 4th King's Own Scottish Borderers in five waves, began to approach Uncle Beach a few minutes before 8:00am. With the beachhead secure Lieutenant-Colonel Melville was confident that his men could make a safe landing. C Company touched down unscathed and the streets echoed to the sounds of Captain David Colville's hunting horn as the commandos assembled behind the dike. B Company landed next, and as the two companies prepared to move out, Captain James Bennett, the support company commander went forward in search of the 4 Commando's headquarters. As Bennett approached Bellamypark, he was severely wounded in the back by a sniper's bullet; the battalion's first casualty.

Meanwhile, the remaining LCAs carrying A, D and HQ Companies approached the shore. This time the Germans were waiting for them. Machine-guns and mortars raked the craft as they hit the beach and although casualties were light, the battalion's communication equipment suffered badly. Both radio links with the mainland were lost on the beach and the battalion control set was damaged beyond repair by shrapnel.

As his men began to organise themselves, Lieutenant-Colonel Melville decided to seek out 4 Commando's headquarters for himself, finding it in Bellamypark. After a quick briefing Melville returned to his men, instructing Captain Colville to take C Company and two carrier sections to Bexhill. Meanwhile, the rest of the battalion would wait in reserve until the bottleneck had been cleared.

C Company reached Bexhill by 10:00am, however, crossfire had turned the junction into a killing zone. 'Dover' strong point at the end of Coosje Buskenstraat was still active and the machine-gun post along Aagje Dekenstraat was equally alert. Any sign of movement in the street was met by bursts of 20mm cannon and machine-gun fire. Captain Colville did not have any heavy weapons to return fire, or the means to make smoke. After despatching a runner to Battalion headquarters, he ordered C Company to take cover.

After hearing Colville's report, Lieutenant-Colonel Melville took steps to reinforce C Company. So far, radio

Troops move cautiously through the ruins.

communications had failed and Melville personally led B Company towards 'Bexhill' to assess the strength of the opposition for himself. He did not have long to wait. Making his way forward along Walstraat, B Company was spotted by a German machine-gun crew at the end of Badhuisstraat. Concentrated fire forced B Company to take cover in side streets and doorways. Melville quickly ordered his men to make their way through the back streets and houses; he now knew for himself that 'Bexhill' was a dangerous place.

Once at Coosje Buskenstraat, Melville could for see himself how the Germans covered the road from every angle and ordered the carrier sections forward to make smoke at two points. Clouds soon filled the street, obscuring the German gunners view, but as a platoon of C Company made the mad dash to the school on the far side. The rest of Colville's company followed, but by the time a platoon of B Company had crossed, the smoke had begun to clear.

For the time being, the position north of Coosje Buskenstraat was secure, increasing the KOSBs grip on 'Bexhill'. Lieutenant-Colonel Melville was confident that his men could hold their perimeter and as time passed, the Scots began to feel the advantage of fire support. Their 3-inch mortars targeted the machine-gun post on Aagje Dekenstraat while the Canadian artillery across the estuary shelled the streets beyond 'Bexhill'. Even so, the German snipers and machine gun teams remained active, making it impossible to send more troops forward. The KOSBs were caught in a stalemate, unable to advance or regroup; all they could do was watch and wait. Meanwhile, the local population tried to escape the battle:

Civilians surprisingly quick in appearing between periods of shelling and other fire – impossible to control them in any great extent – however, the necessity did not arise, since they disciplined themselves admirably.

As the attack developed, members of the local resistance emerged to offer advice but despite their good intentions, the soldiers often found the assistance distracting:

It was found very early that information and assistance from the Underground Army was erratic both in veracity and usefulness. Though their help did increase throughout the action.

As the battle for Flushing slowly degenerated into deadlock,

Lieutenant-Colonel Melville returned to his headquarters in Gravestraat, to consider his next step. Rather than renewing the attack's momentum, half of his battalion was embroiled around 'Bexhill' crossroads. A third company was engaged near 'Dover' alongside 4 Commando. The battalion diary sums up Melville's predicament.

> This sniping, and resistance by isolated machine-guns, extremely difficult to combat owing to Germans' superior knowledge of ground, and ease with which these small bodies could conceal themselves and change position.

At 1:00pm Lieutenant-Colonel Melville finally received a reserve radio set and for the first time, he was able to report to Brigadier McLaren on the far side of the estuary. Now that the 4th KOSBs were fully occupied, the 5th KOSBs would have to take over the lead as soon as they landed.

5th King's Own Scottish Borderers

Lieutenant-Colonel William Turner's men started to embark at 2:00pm, but as A and C Companies set sail, there were growing concerns about the safety of Uncle Beach as the Germans targeted the area with every available mortar and gun. The leading wave of LCAs faced a storm of shrapnel and bullets as it approached the dike and in the words of one coxswain; you could not have fitted a matchbox through that wall of lead. Fearing a disaster, Lieutenant-Commander Vernon ordered his LCAs to return to Breskens making smoke.

The 5th KOSBs headed back towards Breskens, disembarking under shellfire at 15:00pm. As they headed for cover the beach parties on Flushing shore waited anxiously. They were isolated for the time being; it would be dark when the LCAs returned, forcing a serious delay on Brigadier McLaren's timetable.

Meanwhile, Lieutenant-Colonel Melville spent the afternoon trying to improve his grip on the town. Although C Company was trapped on the far side of Coosje Buskenstraat, Captain Colville's men held a secure perimeter. They had managed to capture a quartermaster and cook and the two were put to good use, feeding C Company on German rations.

D Company had reinforced 4 Commando's attack on 'Dover', they had, so far, been unable to reach the strong point. An engineer officer, sent by Melville to assess the situation, had been unable to provide a satisfactory solution. The closest an assault party could get to the bunker under cover was fifty metres; even then, the troops would be forced to emerge via a small window, one at a time. Although a flame-thrower would have been ideal, the Scots had none to hand.

Late in the afternoon 155 Brigade planned to shell 'Dover' with the heavy artillery across the estuary. Withdrawing to a safe distance beyond Spuistraat, the Commandos and Scots waited as the shells targeted the strong point. They had hoped the bombardment would subdue the Germans inside. They were to be disappointed. As 4 Commando edged back towards the seafront 'Dover' opened fire once more. By nightfall they managed to secure a perimeter around Groote Markt and Paarden Markt. The battle for 'Dover' would be renewed the following day.

Meanwhile, A Company of the 4th KOSBs had entered the De Schelde shipbuilding yards, infiltrating the dockyard offices and workshops. It had been hoped that they would be able to increase the hold on 'Bexhill', but they were met with heavy fire at dock gates. Although they could see B Company across the street, the Scots were unable to cross.

Later that evening Battalion headquarters was informed that several dockyard buildings had been booby-trapped and there were concerns that German rearguards would try detonate the demolition charges after dark. It was a risk that Lieutenant-Colonel Melville did not want to take. After withdrawing A Company from the area, a small team began searching the area:

This task extremely difficult: very dark night and exact enemy locations not known; no charges found within limits of search – no building in fact blew up.

At 9:30pm Lieutenant-Colonel Melville received his orders for the following day. The 5th KOSBs had eventually managed to land under cover of darkness. While the 4th KOSBs held their positions, Brigadier McLaren planned to renew the attack on the New Town with the 5th KOSBs. The attack would begin at 5:30am, preceded by an intense bombardment.

As the day ended, the head of the Dutch Underground visited Lieutenant-Colonel Melville's headquarters with worrying news. There had been a large number of civilian casualties during the battle and many had been taken to the hospital at the south-west corner of the De Schelde Aircraft factory. Others had gathered in the building in the hope of escaping the shelling and the resistance leader estimated there were over one thousand men, women and children in the area. Lieutenant-Colonel Melville tried to assure the resistance leader that the artillery would attempt to avoid the hospital. He also promised to try to evacuate as many civilians as possible at first light. In return, Melville asked the Dutch to try to persuade any Germans in the area to surrender. With a promise of fair treatment, should they leave the hospital alongside the Dutch, before the area came under attack.

Brigadier McLaren landed on the island before midnight, joining Lieutenant-Colonel Dawson at his headquarters. Having heard how far 4 Commando had advanced, McLaren issued his orders for the morning. The primary objective was to clear the seafront as far north as 'Dover', releasing many of Dawson's troops. The commandos would attack at first light, targeting 'Brighton', 'Worthing' and 'Dover'.

Later that night everyone was relieved to hear that General Daser, the German commanding officer of the 70th Division and overall commander of the island, had broadcast his willingness to surrender on the Canadian frequency. While Brigadier McLaren was aware that many of those defending the island would follow their commander's lead, some would fight to the last. All units received the following warning in response to the offer:

This would be accepted provided all German positions show the white flag. Corps policy is to respect the white flag strictly. This to be accepted with provision that if any position showing white flag fires upon any sub-unit, drastic action will be taken against it.

Many soldiers knew from bitter experience that the white flag had to be treated with caution.

CHAPTER FIVE

INFATUATE II – ASSAULT ON WESTKAPELLE

In the early hours of 1 November, T Force left Ostend docks on the beginning of a seven-hour journey. While the battle raged in Flushing, the assortment of ships and landing craft ploughed on through a moderate sea, making a huge loop around the mouth of the River Schelde. At first poor weather had led to concerns over the sea-worthiness of some of the landing craft but a reconnaissance by Tom Masterman, Captain Pugsley's chief of staff, brought good news, the sea conditions ahead appeared to be favourable.

As the hours passed, the commandos tried to sleep while the naval crews watched for E-Boats and mines and eventually when dawn broke, Captain Pugsley was relieved to see the coastline ahead. There was no mistake about the location of the landing beaches; Westkapelle lighthouse was directly ahead,

An LCT crammed with Buffaloes and Weasels heads towards Westkapelle as commandos look on anxiously. IWM A26266

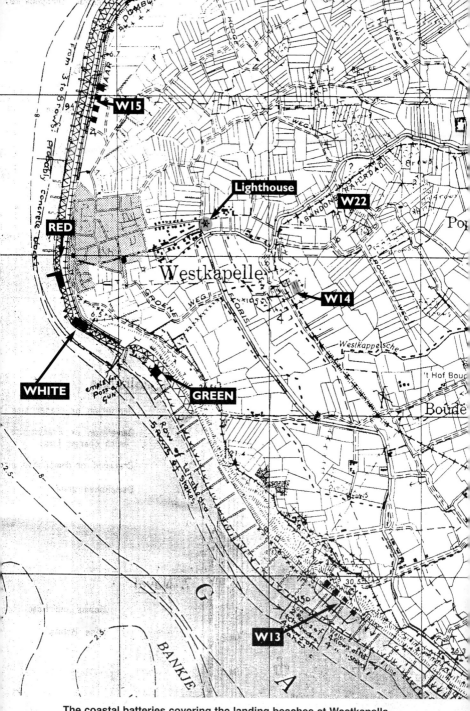

The coastal batteries covering the landing beaches at Westkapelle.

standing proud above the dike 'like a match sticking out of an apple'.

Although the sea conditions were favourable for the landing, there were concerns over the promised air support. Although the skies above the Dutch coast were clear, fog had enveloped the English airfields. As the task force sailed towards its target, Pugsley faced an agonising decision. If the fighters and bombers did not arrive on time, the shore batteries would be able to target the landing craft unhindered. It also meant that the Bombardment Squadron would be deprived of its spotter aircraft, essential for accurate targeting. As Captain Pugsley and Brigadier Leicester watched the coastline from the bridge of HMS *Kingsmill* they both knew that there was little chance of remounting the operation before the end of the year; postponement would mean cancellation of the operation. Agonising minutes passed as the two officers waited for further information about air cover. None came but both men concluded that they had to continue, having come this far. Just before 7:30am Captain Pugsley issued the code word 'Nelson' to his subordinates, Operation INFATUATE II was underway.

Two motor launches sped ahead of T Force to mark the offshore sandbanks, coming within range of the Westkapelle Battery, W15. The guns opened fire on the small launches at precisely 8:09am and the salvo heralded the start of a

The German gun crews had ample time to target the Support Squadron.

tremendous gun battle. Five minutes later, the Bombardment Squadron returned fire, but while HMS *Warspite* targeted Domburg Battery, HMS *Erebus* failed to fire. The turret-training engine had jammed, making it impossible to aim the monitor's guns, the ship would be out of action until the landing was well under way. In the meantime, Captain Marcel Kelsey, the Bombardment Squadron's commanding officer, ordered HMS *Roberts* to fire on *Erebus'* target, the Westkapelle Battery.

W13 Battery, south of the Westkapelle beaches, soon joined the gun battle, targeting the slow moving landing craft as they headed for the shore. While the landing craft carrying 4 Special Service Brigade headed straight for the gap in the dike, Captain Sellar split the Support Squadron into two equal groups to engage targets north and south of Westkapelle. As hoped, the shore batteries turned their attentions on the Support Craft to begin with, rather than the unarmed infantry carrying craft. Despite being seriously outgunned, Sellar's men headed straight for the shore, sailing into a devastating barrage of shells.

Although the two groups engaged the shore batteries simultaneously, it is necessary to take each action in turn.

The Support Squadron – Southern Group

Sailing line abreast, the LCGs led the southern group towards the shore, opening fire on W15 battery with their 4.7" and 17-pounder guns at 10,000m and at intervals. Although huge bursts of smoke and flame indicated hits on the dike, the guns stood little chance of damaging one of the 150mm guns. As the German naval crews returned fire, their shells threw up huge plumes of water among the craft. It would only be a matter of time before they found their range in a long-range duel lasting over an hour.

4,000m from the shore the two rocket firing craft assigned to the southern group began to turn broadside ready to open fire. LCT (R) 363, commanded by Lieutenant Keir Rasmussen RNR, successfully fired its salvo of rockets, straddled the radar station on the dike. Moments later W13 returned the compliment as two six-inch shells tore through the engine room starting a fire. Despite his injuries, Leading Seaman Stanley Winrow led the fire-fighting party as they fought the blaze. Below decks, Chief Motor Mechanic Frank Woods had also been seriously wounded during the blast but he stayed at his post operating the remaining engine by hand. Both men received the DSM for helping to save their stricken craft.

Meanwhile, as LCT (R) 334 turned ready to fire, disaster struck when two of W13's shells hit the ship's magazine. The explosion ignited forty rockets and observers watched anxiously as they fell harmlessly into the sea close to the northern group. Lieutenant Ernest Howard RNVR fought to regain control of the damaged craft and eventually fired the remaining rockets onto their target. However, the crew had little time to congratulate themselves as W13 again found its target. Burning fiercely, LCT (R) 334 turned out to sea as the crew fought the fire.

Before long, LCT (R) 363's surviving engine failed and as the rest of the Support Craft went into action LCT (R) 334 gave a tow to its stricken sister ship. The two craft eventually limped back to Ostend.

Meanwhile, the rest of the Southern Group sailed towards the shoreline. The three LCG (L)s of Lieutenant David Crealock's Flotilla opened fire first, targeting the southern shoulder of the gap with their 6-pounder guns. Although seriously out-gunned, the three craft fired steadily at their targets while salvo after salvo straddled the slow moving craft. It was only a matter of time before the German guns found their mark. LCG (L) 10 was hit first, set on fire by a 6-inch shell. Struggling to regain control, Lieutenant Clifford Holbrook manoeuvred his craft so that the flames did not fan the bridge. Once the crew had brought the fire under control, Holbrook turned his craft back on course. As LCG (L) 10 headed once more towards the shore the surviving crew members formed two scratch gun teams. As the craft came into range, Lieutenant James Harvie RM discovered that the communication cables connecting the bridge and the gun turrets had been cut by exploding ammunition. Harvie supervised the crews, running from turret to turret to sight each gun in turn. Over the next four hours LCG (L) 10 fired more than 525 rounds of high explosive.

LCG (L) 11 was hit twice in quick succession. The first salvo of shells struck the bridge, and while Lieutenant Thomas Foggitt RANVR struggled to steer the stricken craft away from the shore, a second salvo hit the engine room. Foggitt collapsed soon after, and the senior able officer, Sub-Lieutenant John

Landing craft carrying 4 Special Brigade sail towards the gap in the dike.

Smith, took control of the damaged craft. Once the crew had brought the fires under control, Smith steered LCG (L) 11 back towards the coastline. Before long both turrets commenced firing over open sights, supervised by Corporal James Jackson.

Having seen the damage wrought by W13, Lieutenant George Ring RNR took evasive action, piloting LCG (L) 9 through a barrage of shells. Laying smoke as it sailed along the coast, the weaving craft led a charmed life as it targeted bunkers south of the gap. Despite the full attentions of W13's guns, LCG (L) 9 survived the battle. Lieutenant Crealock's men continued to fight on from their damaged craft throughout the landing but the battle cost LCG (L) group dearly; fifty-five crewmen were killed drawing fire from the commandos' landing craft.

Three LCS (L) craft escorted the largest craft in the group, LCG (M) 102, as it sailed towards W266, a pillbox position covering 'White' Beach. A salvo of shells from W13 soon hit the first in line, LCS (L) 252, and the explosions ignited the petrol tanks, blowing the fragile craft sky high. Minutes later shells struck LCS (L) 256, setting it on fire. Lieutenant Sidney Orum acted immediately, drawing alongside the stricken ship in LCS (L) 258 to rescue the survivors. Shells soon targeted the two stationary craft turning them into burning hulks. As fires burned out of control, calls to abandon ship came too late to save many. As men jumped into the sea, the stricken ships exploded in sheets of flame; there were only a handful of survivors.

Once it had dealt with the three LCS (L) craft, W13 turned its attentions on LCG (M) 102. Close to the shore, the craft received a direct hit forward of the control position but the blast failed to deter Lieutenant Donald Flory RNVR. Refusing to take evasive action Flory sailed on, beaching opposite his target at 09:43am. The 17-pounders fired repeatedly at W266, and although the shells hit time after time, they failed to penetrate the thick concrete. Flory's crewmen could see that they were unable to destroy the bunker but they remained at their posts in the hope of distracting the Germans inside. Dozens of shells slammed into the stationary craft and while the gun crews engaged their target, the rest of the crew fought fires. LCG (M) 102 continued to draw fire as 48 Commandos' landing craft sailed by towards White Beach. The marines looked on horrified as the burning craft eventually exploded in sheets of flame. All thirty-two of Flory's crewmen perished.

As 48 Commando's landing craft made the final run in to the gap, the three LCF landing craft opened fire with their 2-pounder guns and Oerlikons. The puny weapons stood little chance of destroying anything but the crews stuck to their task, firing on any target in sight. The ruse worked and while the LCFs drew fire from every gun in range, 48 Commando's craft remained unharmed. Their was, however, a terrible price to pay. Shell after shell struck LCF 37 and the debriefing report describes the craft's final moments:

*She was first hit on the port quarter on the water line at 9:20,
but the hole was successfully blocked with hammocks. At 9:45,
W15 having switched to fresh targets, she was engaged by W13
and began to make smoke. However, she was hit astern, a near
miss on the port beam filled the bridge and upper deck with
water, and two hits were sustained forward blowing away the
bows and forward magazine. At 09:48 a shell hit the main
magazine, blowing up about 100,000 rounds of 2pdr and
Oerlikon ammunition, turning the ship forward of the bridge
into a shambles and causing a large number of casualties. Most
of the crew were blown into the sea.*

After LCF 37 disintegrated, W13 turned its attentions on LCF 32
and LCF 35. Despite numerous hits and near misses the craft led
charmed lives. As the landing proceeded Captain Sellar ordered
the two close in to support the landing. LCF 32 was finally hit
below the waterline and although the stricken craft fought on
the flooding caused irreparable damage to the engines. LCF 32
eventually came to its aid, towing its sister ship to safety.

The Support Squadron – Northern Group

While the southern group fought a losing battle with W13,
the northern group engaged targets north of the gap in the dike.
Again the three LCG (L)s led the group into action, but soon
after they opened fire on W15 Battery and Westkapelle
lighthouse, disaster struck. The three rocket craft attached to the
group had swung into position unharmed but as LCT (R) 457
opened fire, its rockets fell short landing harmlessly in the sea.
LCT (R) 378 fired next and the officers on HMS *Kingsmill*
watched in horror as the salvo also fell short, showering the
northern group with missiles. The LCG (L) took evasive action,
emerging unscathed but some of the rockets hit LCF 42,
wounding thirty-three men and setting the craft on fire. As
Lieutenant Francis Keep struggled to keep his craft on course,
the depleted crew fought to bring the blaze under control.
Despite the catastrophe, LCF 42 eventually went into action
with scratch gun teams. LCG (L) 2 was also hit by rockets, losing
power for a short time. Although his crew suffered casualties,
Lieutenant Martin Ward's craft was soon back in action. The
third rocket ship, LCT (R) 331 fired its salvo a few minutes later
and to everyone's relief, the rockets fell on their intended target;
Westkapelle.

A range finder bunker, responsible for co-ordinating accurate fire.
H Houterman

After their fright, the three LCG (L) craft swung back into line heading for the northern shoulder of the gap. W15 Battery posed the main threat to the Northern Group and its 6-inch guns soon found their range. Lieutenant Alfred Ballard's craft, LCG (L) 1, was the first to suffer damage when two shells set the craft on fire. The explosions wounded many of the crew including every officer on board. In the chaos that followed, the injured Ballard steered the craft towards the shore while Captain G Penney shouted instructions through a gaping hole in the deck to the gun crews below. Ballard eventually collapsed leaving Penney to take command of the damaged craft. The craft eventually lost power near the beach, leaving the crew to the mercy of the German guns.

Lieutenant Arthur Cheney chose a different tactic to engage targets on the dike. By piloting LCG (L) 2 right up to the shoreline, he brought his craft under the elevation of W15's guns. However, while his own crew engaged targets on the dike, two 88mm guns fired at point blank range into the craft, damaging the engine room. While crewmembers worked below decks, frantically plugging holes with blankets and hammocks, LCG (L) 2 fought a losing battle with the German guns. Eventually, Cheney decided he could do no more and turned away from the shore. A shell slammed into the bridge as it made the manoeuvre, injuring many of the crew. The coxswain, Petty

Officer Arthur Harris survived the explosion and managed to guide the stricken craft out to sea.

Meanwhile, LCG (L) 17 fought a running battle with W15, weaving along the coast to draw fire from the rest of the squadron. Despite a number of hits the craft survived and it was eventually recalled having expended most of its ammunition.

The fragile LCS (L) came next and the flotilla commander, Lieutenant Edward Howell, ordered his ships to zig-zag along the coastline at full speed. Although the three craft managed to sail in to the beach several times, their guns were powerless against the pillboxes on the dike. Eventually, a shell found its target, hitting Howell's own craft, LCS (L) 260. The blast destroyed the engine, leaving the damaged ship helpless on the beach. As Leading Motor Mechanic William Cheeney set about tackling a fire, Lieutenant Eric Tiplady guided LCS (L) 259 alongside to assist. The crews managed to rig up a tow and under heavy fire the two craft pulled away from the shore, while LCS (L) 260 continued to burn fiercely. Once out of danger, Tiplady cast off and manoeuvred into position to help his sister ship with his own fire hoses. As LCS (L) 259 circled around the burning craft, the crew was surprised to see Cheeney sitting in a shell-hole above petrol tanks. Fully aware that 2,600 gallons of fuel beneath his feet could explode at any moment Cheeney had continued to fight the blaze. After rigging a hose between the two craft, he returned to his perch, eventually bringing the fire under control. Cheeney's bravery saved LCS (L) 260 from destruction and he was later awarded the CGM for his actions.

LCG (M) 101 sails towards Westkapelle as rockets land short of their target. IWM A26240

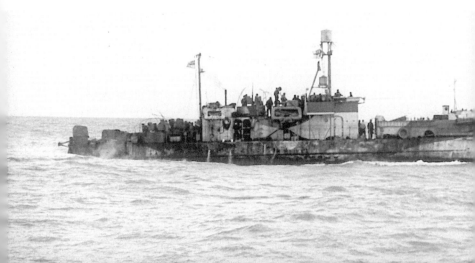

LCS (L) 254 sailed at high speed along the shore, engaging pillboxes overlooking the landing area and despite dozens of near misses, the craft emerged unscathed. Sub-Lieutenant George Kirk eventually pulled alongside the powerless LCG (L) 1, stranded on the beach. Under heavy fire, the two crews managed to attach a tow but LCS (L) 254 found the load too heavy. Captain Penney, realising his craft was beyond help, ordered his men to abandon ship and scramble onto the smaller craft. The order was given just in time. As LCS (L) 254 pulled away from the shore LCG (L) 1 erupted in flames.

Lieutenant George Flamank piloted LCG (M) 101 straight towards the shore through a barrage of shells from W15, eventually beaching within thirty metres of his target, W267. Once ashore, the landing craft drew fire from every quarter:

> ... the forward arc of the ship appears to have been out of the arc of the guns of W15, but further aft many hits in the port side were sustained although nothing penetrated the armoured portion. B turret was eventually put out of action by small arms fire entering the sighting slots and A turret by a splinter, which bounced of the deck and damaged the recuperator. It was estimated that some fifty rounds of ammunition were expended.

With his guns out of action, Flamank gave orders to withdraw from the beach. While the ballast tanks emptied, crewmen emerged from below decks to operate the kedge, a winch used to retract the craft from shore. The first on deck were killed as they tried to operate the winch but others took their place allowing the ship to sail full astern. However, as it pulled away it was clear to Flamank that LCG (M) 101 was in desperate trouble. Shells had peppered the stern with holes. Sinking fast,

An LCG (M), in this case LCG (M) 101, begins to sink. IWM A26240

LCG (M) 101 begins to capsize. IWM A26233

LCG (M) 101 capsized. TAYLOR LIBRARY

the ship's steering and gyro failed in quick succession. As the stricken craft keeled over, the crew abandoned ship, jumping into the sea. Many clambered onto the overturned hull, helping wounded comrades out of the icy water; they were eventually rescued by a passing LCS (I). Lieutenant George Flamank was awarded the DSC for commanding LCG (M) 101 during its suicidal attack.

As 41 Commando's landing craft made their final approach towards Red and White Beaches, the three LCF sailed close in to the shore to draw fire. Lieutenant-Commander Frank Lammert's men fired thousands of rounds against the bunkers, on the northern shoulder of the gap, in the hope of distracting

LCIs beached on Red Beach. TAYLOR LIBRARY

the occupants inside. Lieutenant Keep's scratch crew had manned LCF 42's guns following the earlier rocket strike and in spite of several hits his craft engaged targets throughout the morning. Meanwhile, LCF 38 commanded by Lieutenant Alfred Wilks, drew the most attention. The magazine was hit at the outset and further shells destroyed the wheelhouse, killing the officers and coxswain. Able Seaman Crothers eventually reached the shattered bridge and after pulling the bodies of his officers from the wheel, took control of the crippled ship. The craft continued to engage targets under the command of

Buffaloes 'swim' the last leg, heading for White Beach. IWM A26272

Corporal William Miller, but further hits soon reduced LCF 38 to a shambles. Although the other's called for assistance, by the time LCF 36 drew alongside LCF 38's magazine was ablaze. After transferring ship, the survivors were evacuated to HMS *Kingsmill*. Lieutenant Norman Ellams eventually towed the burning LCF 38 out to sea.

Lieutenant-Commander Frank Lammert's flotilla was virtually destroyed, and the Support Squadron was also all but destroyed engaging the German guns at Westkapelle. The ferocity of the coastal batteries had shocked everyone. Lieutenant James Harvie commented how his craft had fired more than one and a half times as much ammunition than it had during six days at Normandy. Of twenty-five craft, ten had been sunk and six were beyond repair. While a few craft continued to engage targets on the dunes, the rest limped to safety, joining the 'Crock' fleet heading for Ostend.

Sellar's men had paid a heavy price by sailing in close to the shore to engage the shore batteries and pillboxes on the dike: 172 were killed or missing at sea and 125 had been wounded. In recognition of their bravery, one hundred and

Buffaloes and Weasels drive ashore onto White Beach. IWM A26271

The first wave landed on Red Beach, subsequent waves sailed through the gap to land on the inner flanks of the dike.

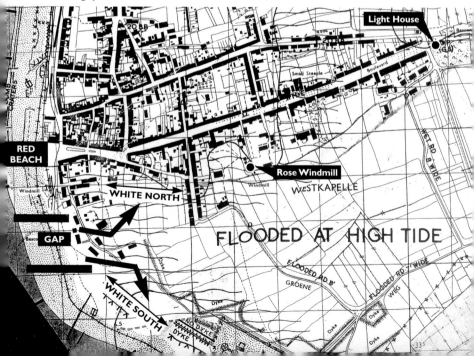

thirty officers and men received recommendations for awards. The awards panel considered which medals would be appropriate. The First Sea Lord suggested that there should be nominees for the Victoria Cross. Also he offered the opinion that there ought to be more nominated for the Conspicuous Gallantry Medal than shortlisted. Despite further investigations, the awards panel did not act on either suggestion.

4 Special Service Brigade's Landings

While the German guns targeted the support craft, the first wave of landing craft sailed towards Red Beach and for a time it seemed that the landing was in grave danger of failing. However, as often happens in warfare, fate took a turn in favour of 4 Special Service Brigade:

> ... about the time when the first landing craft were going inshore nearly half an hour late, there occurred what was probably the most important single event of the operation. The undamaged battery W13, which could engage craft sometimes at only 2,000 to 3,000 yards range, ran out of ammunition for its four 150mm guns.

Later investigations discovered that the battery was isolated by the floodwater and had been unable to restock its depleted supply of ammunition. Poor fire discipline had saved the Commandos landing craft from destruction.

As if on cue, Typhoons and Spitfires flew low over the task force, strafing targets along the dike as 41 Commando's first wave touched down on Red Beach. In spite of the poor weather conditions over England, 84th Group RAF had managed to fulfil its promise. Arthur Oakeshott, Reuter's Special Correspondent, watched the landing from HMS *Kingsmill*:

> By this time several landing craft were burning fiercely, it was not pretty. Then I saw an unforgettable sight – dozens of landing craft bearing hundreds of men wearing green berets – the men of the famous Royal Marines. They were all singing, yes singing, going through that hell of fire and shell and flying metal... This was not a kid glove war and this is what I saw – horror upon horror, burning craft, craft battered and smashed, and dying men, and fighting men and men of courage beyond all belief.

Once ashore, B Troop occupied the crest of the dike unopposed, while the machine-gun and mortar sections took up supporting positions. Meanwhile, P Troop turned north to engage W15 Battery. The commandos began targeting the control tower with small arms fire, hoping to distract the gunnery officers inside.

A few minutes later, the first two LCTs carrying the armoured support approached Red Beach. A salvo of shells from W15 straddled the leading craft, *Damson*, 400 metres from the shore. Lieutenant P Martin's RNVR report details the damage:

> Hits were made as follows on the craft, one on the port ramp winch, one about half way down the port side, one on the wheel house. On AVRE T/172071; one on the base of the Petard at the mounting and one on the Fascine setting it alight. On AVRE T/68399; one on a bridge girder, probably another on the hoisting cable which caused the bridge to drop on a Flail tank ahead of it in the craft. There may have been additional hits because the jibs on all the flails were damaged.

Although there were only half a dozen casualties, the shells had ripped the waterproofing on many of the tanks and started a menacing fire. Lieutenant Martin was forced to turn his craft

41 Commando head towards Westkapelle's lighthouse. IWM B11638

away from the beach to assess the damage. A fascine on one of the AVRE tanks had been set on fire, endangering the ammunition lockers. Lance-Sergeant Black set about tackling the fire, but his attempt was hampered without a fire hose; the shells had also cut the landing craft's water line. While some ferried water to the fire, others cleared the lockers of ammunition. A second landing craft, *Apple*, pulled alongside to help, but its fire hoses were useless, having been shot to pieces. Lieutenant Martin was ordered to return to Ostend with his crippled cargo soon afterwards.

W15's next target was *Cherry*, and the first shell struck the landing craft's stern, damaging the engine room. Another shell collapsed an AVRE's bridging equipment on top of a flail tank. Despite the heavy fire, Lieutenant Chamberlain sailed close in to Red Beach. When the ramp dropped, the tank crews found to their dismay that the beach consisted of loose cobbles and shingle, far from ideal for tracked vehicles. After several failed attempts to land his cargo, Lieutenant Norman Chamberlain RNVR was ordered to withdraw and join the remaining two LCTs. Lieutenant-Commander Bernard Arbuthnot had decided to re-route his remaining craft onto White Beach, away from W15's deadly guns.

As the landing progressed on Red Beach, the second wave of landing craft, carrying the rest of 41 Commando, sailed through the gap in the dike. The two leading LCTs safely landed their cargo on the south side of the gap. Once ashore, A Troop and X Troop crossed the fast flowing channel in their Buffaloes to attack Westkapelle. A Troop dismounted from their vehicles on the southern edge of village, and began working their way quickly through the ruins. Meanwhile, X Troop followed in echelon, advancing down the main street.

With the western edge of the village secure, Lieutenant-Colonel Eric Palmer ordered P Troop forward from the dike so they could clear the northern outskirts of the village; B Troop proceeded to mop up behind. Resistance was virtually non-existent and the flooding had turned Westkapelle into a ghost town:

> 'Bombing had reduced the seaward half of the town to complete ruin and the force of the sea had swamped the wrecks of the houses, so all that remained were gigantic bomb craters, half filled with water upon which the pitiful sodden remains of

Lieutenant-Colonel Laycock and Major Franks eventually reach the beach.

furniture were floating. The destruction was the most terrible we had seen anywhere, and one felt that human beings ought not be able to cause such havoc.

Two troops of 10 (Inter-Allied) Commando followed 41 Commando onto White Beach. Two sub-sections of the Belgian troop had accompanied the 1st Lothian's, to act as protection for the tanks. The sight of *Bramble* landing craft heading for home with Captain Joy's sub-section, having been damaged by W15 guns 'was not an aid for morale'. The LCT carrying Lieutenant-Colonel Peter Laycock's Headquarters struck an obstacle close to the shoreline and for ten agonising minutes the naval crew struggled in vain to free the craft. Diving overboard into the icy water, the commandos waded ashore, leaving their Buffaloes and Weasels behind. The next LCT also hit under water obstacles. Although the coxswain wanted to try and land closer, Lieutenant Dauppe asked to land immediately before the Germans targeting the craft began to cause casualties. Driving ashore, the Belgians quickly dealt with the opposition with their Bren guns. The unit war diary sums up 10 Commando's landing.

Landing very wet, strong current and deep water, with

mortar and shell fire to add to the confusion. Casualties, however, were light.

As 41 Commando and 10 Commando made their way through Westkapelle, 48 Commando's men braced themselves for the landing on White Beach.

As the first wave of landing craft carrying 48 Commando sailed through the gap, the marines targeted the Radar Station W154 with every gun they had. Three landing craft touched down on White Beach a couple of minutes after 41 Commando and made their way up the beach. Although shells plastered the beach, casualties had been light and it appeared that the Germans had already withdrawn from the bunkers overlooking the beach.

B Troop went forward first, finding the pillboxes on the southern shoulder of the gap empty, X Troop took over the advance, finding the radar station deserted. For the first time the commandos came under small arms fire and without delay, X Troop made a search of the area, taking a few prisoners. Moving along the dunes overlooking Green Beach, X Troop

Escorting prisoners along Westkapelle's main street. IWM B11637

quickly overran the group of bunkers known as W285. The garrison of the next strongpoint, W286, surrendered without a fight.

While the lead troops worked their way along the dike, the second wave of landing craft approached White Beach under heavy fire. Major Wilfred Sendall's few words give an insight into how fierce the German reaction was:

> Most of the marines landed early in the assault on Normandy and all of them thought that this little D-Day was far more terrifying than the big one.

Two LCTs received direct hits and turned away while their crews battled with fires onboard. A third struck a line of hidden stakes short of the shore and the Buffaloes were quickly swamped as they drove off the ramp into deep water. Although the men could swim ashore, they lost a large amount of equipment in the calamity. Another LCT received direct hits close to the shore. One shell damaged the machine-gun section's Buffalo beyond repair and although casualties were light, the crews had to manhandle their equipment ashore.

As the commandos struggled ashore, artillery fire plastered the crowded beach. Two Buffaloes loaded with ammunition

An LCT comes under fire as its load of Buffaloes and Weasels drive onto White Beach. IWM A26268

An AVRE Bulldozer makes its way off the beach, as a line of Buffaloes comes ashore. IWM B11647

received direct hits and the following explosions caused by the blazing ammunition caused havoc on the beach. Mines also took their toll on the Buffaloes and Weasels as their drivers struggled to manoeuvre their vehicles around huge bomb craters. The combination of shells, mines and mud accounted for all but a handful of vehicles. Captain Noel Godkin, 48 Commando's adjutant, worked tirelessly to keep order, guiding men to their assembly points. During the morning he was mortally wounded by a mortar shell, and died a few days later in an Ostend hospital.

As the landing progressed, Beachmaster Commander Redvers Prior and his team battled to keep White Beach clear. The shore line was far from ideal and the coxswains of the landing craft faced thick mud, huge bomb craters and burning vehicles before they could land their cargo. One craft became stranded, blocking the easiest exit from the beach as its crew struggled to free it from the mud.

As the marines struggled ashore, the three remaining landing craft carrying the armoured assault teams added to the chaos. LCT *Bramble* landed first and the leading Sherman flail tank, bogged down as soon as it hit the beach. The bridge-laying AVRE managed to position its equipment but it too became stuck as it drove off the far end of the bridge. *Apple*, the second of the LCT's carrying tanks, met similar difficulties:

> *Craft touched down at 1100 hrs and leading flails went ashore and immediately bogged down on soft clay. Crew drew off and came back in ten yards to the north of bogged flails. The two other flails went off and also bogged. Realised that ground on which ramp was touching was no use for landing. Brought forward bridge AVRE and dropped bridge from ramp of LCT on to what I thought looked hard ground twenty-five feet from ship. This ground was misleading as AVRE after running over bridge immediately bogged in it. Fascine AVRE thinking we had got onto solid ground came on to bridge and LCT backed away.*

Cherry, eventually reached the crowded beach and all the tanks except one flail, trapped under the fallen AVRE bridge, managed to get ashore. As the tanks made their way up the beach a bulldozer unearthed a mine, losing a track in the explosion.

Attempts to tow the bogged tanks to safety were eventually beaten by the rising tide. As mortar shells crashed down men struggled to attach tow ropes to the stricken vehicles. The rescue was eventually abandoned when waves started to wash over the turrets forcing the crews to swim to shore.

As the tanks crawled up the beach, AQMS Evans REME and Sergeant Hickson (Lothians) organised a party of men, working hard to clear a way through the maze of obstacles. Sergeant Ferguson's flail led the column of tanks to the top of the dike as 41 Commando was nearing the far end of Westkapelle. Although the village had been deserted, A Troop came under fire as it approached the lighthouse. In response to a call for fire support, Sergeant Ferguson's crew fired eleven rounds into the lighthouse tower. CSM Stockell targeted the door with his PIAT and small arms fire followed in the hope of subduing the men inside. During a cease fire Sergeant Freddy Gray and Corporal Maurice Latimer (interpreters attached from 10 (Inter-Allied) Commando) managed to coax the Germans out.

Having cleared Westkapelle, Lieutenant-Colonel Eric Palmer ordered X Troop across the flooded fields to investigate W14 and W22, two battery positions east of the village. Before long he was pleased to hear from Major Paddy Brind-Sheridan that the bunkers had been abandoned, made inhabitable by the seawater.

At 11:15 am, just over an hour after landing, Lieutenant-Colonel Eric Palmer reported that Westkapelle was secure and as 41 Commando took stock of its position, the tanks set about making a road into the village. While the two command Shermans and three flails waited at the top of the dike the 'funnies' set to work with their fascines and bridging equipment. A huge bomb crater blocked the road at the foot of the dike but after AVREs demolished a house, the bulldozers filled the crater with rubble. It had been a difficult journey and although 4 Special Service Brigade had lost over half its supporting armour, the commandos were relieved to see tanks rumbling through Westkapelle.

German guns had begun to find their range by the time the

four LCT's carrying 47 Royal Marine Commando came into land. Two craft suffered hits on the run-in, but the main calamity affected the leading craft carrying Lieutenant-Colonel Farndale Phillips and B Troop. A chance shell struck the leading Buffalo as the ramp lowered. The explosion damaged a Weasel carrying flame-throwing equipment and the port side of the craft erupted in flames. Many leapt overboard and as B Troop attempted to save their wounded from the water, Lance-Sergeant W G Malcolm RE drove the burning vehicle into

Lieutenant-Colonel Phillips.

German guns had the range by the time 47 Royal Marine Commando approached the beaches. This is a German 50mm anti-tank gun.

the water. It was an inauspicious start to 47 Commando's Landing.

Although the second and third landing craft landed safely, the two troops found themselves on the wrong side of the gap. The final LCT managed to reach the correct beach unscathed, but in the confusion the troop commander re-routed his vehicles across the gap. 47 Commando's landing had been a disaster. Three troops were north of the gap, while their commander was to the south with the survivors of B Troop. 47 Commando had suffered thirty casualties, and it would take Lieutenant-Colonel Phillips hours to unravel the chaos. The commandos also found to their cost that the smaller Weasels had failed to cope with the fast rip tide. Seventeen out of twenty Weasels had floundered as they tried to cross the gap, a serious loss of equipment and transport.

At 12:05 am Brigadier Bernard Leicester came ashore, setting up his command post in the abandoned radar station overlooking the gap. Although the most dangerous phase of Operation INFATUATE II was over, there were still serious obstacles to overcome before the beachhead was secure. Abandoned and damaged vehicles littered White Beach and

Lieutenant-Colonel Hope (GSO 1 4 Special Service Brigade), Lieutenant-Colonel Palmer (GOC 41 Commando), Brigadier Leicester with helmet (GOC 4 Special Service Brigade) and Major Wood (41 Commando's second in command) IWM B11634

although the immediate area had been cleared of German troops, coastal batteries still targeted the crowded area. As Brigadier Leicester considered his next move, the final waves of landing craft began to land on Green Beach, bringing stores and equipment.

As 4 Special Service Brigade began the next stage of its operation, many commandos would count themselves lucky to have survived. As one wounded man told the Reuter's correspondent, Arthur Oakeshott,

Don't tell them at home it was easy – it was damn difficult, but we did it – please tell them that.

41 Royal Marine Commando attack W15, the Westkapelle Battery

Having cleared Westkapelle, Lieutenant-Colonel Palmer was able to concentrate on his next objective, W15. The battery lined the Domburg road, north-east of the village and although P Troop had been engaging the casements for some time, the Germans refused to withdraw. The approach along the dunes was too exposed and Palmer took Captain Peter Haydon, Y Troop's commanding officer, along the foot of the dike to find a safer approach.

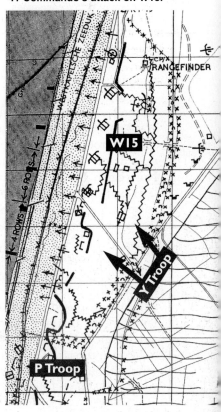

41 Commando's attack on W15.

The Norwegian Troop of 10 (Inter-Allied) Commando joined P Troop on the dunes, adding to the weight of fire directed on the battery. Meanwhile, Y Troop crept closer to the rear of the position. At 12:00 noon Haydon's commandos charged up the dunes under cover of smoke, spreading out among the casemates. The gun crews had no stomach for close quarter fighting and they surrendered as soon as the marines entered the bunkers. Within thirty minutes one hundred prisoners had

The ruins of W15's casemates, destroyed after the battle. H Houterman

been taken, making the beachhead a far safer place. As the commandos searched the casemates they grimly noted that the guns were of British origin, captured in 1940 during the British retreat to Dunkirk.

With the battery secure, Brigadier Leicester ordered Palmer to halt. Although Domburg Battery was still shelling Westkapelle, Leicester wanted to secure Green Beach before sending troops north. The pause allowed 41 Commando to take up a defensive perimeter north of the village. The Belgian and Norwegian Troops of 10 (Inter-Allied) Commando joined them later and the Norwegians took over responsibility for the area surrounding W15. Before long their national flag was to be seen flying above one of the casemates.

48 Royal Marine Commando attack W13 Battery

While 41 Commando dealt with W15, 48 Commando pushed south along the dunes towards their next objective, W13. The battery still posed a serious danger to the T Force, targeting landing craft carrying supplies with its four 150mm guns and two 75mm guns. After fighting running battles along the dunes, Y Troop approached the perimeter of the battery just before 1:00 pm. Although it had been impossible to arrange any fire support, Major Derek de Stacpoole decided to rush the perimeter fence. Running as fast as they could through the drifting sand, Y Troop charged through the minefield but without heavy fire support the charge was nothing short of suicidal. A hail of bullets met the commandos, killing their commander and wounding many of the section leaders.

While Y Troop regrouped, 48 Commando's commanding officer, Lieutenant-Colonel James Moulton, was desperately trying to contact the ships offshore to arrange fire support. He had lost his own radios during the landing, either damaged by shrapnel or sea water. Captain Blunt, the Support Squadron's observer, managed to rescue his radio after shrapnel struck down his operators. Once at the radio station, he was able to contact Captain Sellar onboard HMS *Kingsmill*. Although the Support Squadron had little to offer, the few surviving craft were re-arming, Moulton was able to provide a useful progress report to the headquarters ship.

Captain Arthur Davis, the Bombardment Squadron's observer, reported to the radar station soon afterwards and he was ordered to find Y Troop in the hope of arranging supporting fire. Davis found the commandos near W13's casemates and quickly established contact with HMS *Roberts*. However, the commandos' support was soon cut short; a mortar bomb killed Davis and his wireless operator after only two salvoes. Lieutenant David Winser MC, 48 Commando's medical officer, was also killed.

Radio contact was finally established when Brigadier Leicester's headquarters came ashore

48 Commando's advance along the dunes to W13 Battery.

and with the help of Captain Skelton, the Canadian Artillery observer, contact was established with the guns across the estuary. Although precious time had been lost in the fight for W13, Skelton eventually managed to organise a fire-plan via the brigade radio set.

During the delay, 48 Commando had established a firing position close to W13 but as they waited snipers and mortar fire began to take their toll. X Troop's commanding officer, Captain Roderick Mackenzie, was severely wounded in the head as he made his way back to headquarters. He died a few days later in an Ostend hospital.

When news came through that support fire had been arranged Z Troop prepared to assault, but thirty minutes before zero hour disaster struck. A mortar shell landed amongst the command group, killing nineteen-year-old Lieutenant Cyril Lindrea and injuring Captain Tom Nuttall and Lieutenant John Square. A single shell had left Z Troop leaderless and with no one above corporal capable of walking unaided, Nuttall hobbled across to find B Troop. As he briefed Captain Edwin Teddy Dunn, B Troop took up position on the dunes. Meanwhile, Captain Daniel Flunder had formed a firing line inland of the battery, silencing the troublesome mortars. Despite the disastrous start to its preparations, 48 Commando was ready to attack.

At 3:45pm, the whole weight of the First Canadian Army's artillery began pounding W13. Although the text book called for a wide safety margin during long range artillery shoots, B Troop crawled as close as they dared, fearing the German machine-guns more than their own shells. Fifteen minutes later, Typhoons streaked in across the estuary guided by smoke shells and the commandos hugged the ground as the rockets smashed into the battery. Before the dust had settled, B Troop charged across the minefield, while A Troop provided supporting fire. Fortunately, for Dunn's men many mines had been rendered useless by drifting sand. Even so the marines cursed the sand, Major Sendall summed up the difficult conditions afterwards:

> I must ask you to imagine what it was like, struggling through soft sand that clogged rifles and machine-guns and filled your mouth, eyes and hair.

The German machine-guns came alive as the commandos broke through the perimeter fence and as Lieutenant Peter Allbut struggled with the barbed wire, a German emerged to take aim. Both tried to fire, but the wet sand had jammed their weapons and Allbut threw the useless Sten gun at his enemy in frustration. As Allbut scrambled over the wire, Sergeant John Stringer came to his aid, shooting the German.

A German position silenced.

In spite of heavy casualties, B Troop entered the battery position and quickly cleared two casemates, while X Troop followed in support. Moving forward, the commandos reached the control tower, firing through the observation slits to subdue the Germans inside. As Captain Stephanus Fouché led Y Troop along the beach, W13's garrison began to surrender to Captain Dunn's men. Seventy men, including the battery commander and his second-in-command, were quickly taken prisoner but as Captain Fouché's men patrolled the casemates, a flak cannon opened fire at the far end of the battery. The crew of the anti-aircraft gun soon discovered that the weapon could not depress low enough to trouble the commandos and in frustration they vented their anger on the battery's radar tower.

By sheer determination, 48 Commando had managed to silence W13 and Lieutenant-Colonel Moulton had reason to be proud of his men. For the loss of seven killed and eighty wounded, his men had survived a dangerous landing and secured the southern side of the beachhead. Although it may have been prudent to continue the advance, Moulton recognised that his marines were tired and ammunition supplies were running low. 48 Commando would head towards Zoutelande at first light.

41 Royal Marine Commando advance from Westkapelle to Domburg

Once he had secured artillery support for the attack on W13, Brigadier Leicester turned his attentions to W17, the Domburg

Battery. He hoped that 41 Commando could silence the battery before dark and at 3:00 pm, Lieutenant-Colonel Eric Palmer received instructions to advance north east.

As Y Troop made its way along the dunes, P Troop trudged along the flooded road at the foot of the dike with B Troop in support. The rest of 41 Commando remained at Westkapelle, manhandling stores off the beach. As they marched the commandos were met by dozens of Germans wishing to surrender, but Lieutenant-Colonel Palmer was anxious to `keep moving, sending the prisoners back with the minimum of guards. As the marines moved closer to W17 they watched as twenty-four Spitfires targeted the casemates with 500lb bombs, returning to strafe the battery with their cannons and machine-guns. W283, a smaller strong point covering the road, received similar attention. As 41 Commando approached the casemates with trepidation they were delighted to be met by groups of Germans anxious to surrender.

While B Troop searched the captured battery, Palmer ordered his second-in-command, Major Peter Wood, to reconnoitre Domburg with P Troop. Edging slowly forward the marines again encountered dozens of Germans willing to surrender. Even so progress was slow and by the time P Troop entered the village darkness had fallen. Although there were isolated shots among the burning buildings, it appeared that the main body of Germans had withdrawn into the woods to the east.

While P Troop searched the village, Major Paddy Brind-Sheridan led his men along the sea front. As the light failed, X Troop stumbled on a German strong point and in the ensuing fire-fight Major Brind-Sheridan fell wounded. Once they had pulled back to regroup the commandos noticed that their leader was missing. As patrols tried to locate the injured Major, Lieutenant-Colonel Palmer took steps to seal off the strong point. As B Troop moved forward to the sea front a few Germans broke for cover, hoping to enter the village; they were cut down by a fusillade of shots.

By nightfall 41 Commando had the situation under control. Although they had not completely cleared Domburg, it appeared that the Germans had withdrawn from the ruins. During the early hours of 2 November, Lieutenant-Colonel Palmer joined B Troop on the dunes to assess the troublesome strong point. As he led a patrol along the sea front, Palmer was

met with a distressing scene. Major-Brind-Sheridan and one of his men were found, close to the German wire and although they were still alive, Palmer was unable to go to their assistance. The Germans had lit fires to illuminate their perimeter fence, making it too dangerous to attempt a rescue. As he returned to X Troop Palmer considered his next step, an attack at first light.

As 41 Commando prepared to attack the strong point, the Germans decided to evacuate their position, retiring along the dunes under fire from B Troop. Moving forward cautiously the marines occupied the position to make a tragic discovery. Although the injured marine had survived the night, Major Brind-Sheridan had succumbed to his wounds. However, X Troop had little time to grieve for their leader. Brigadier Leicester was anxious to reach Flushing as soon as possible and he wanted 41 Commando to support the advance south. In the meantime, 10 (Inter-Allied) Commando would take over responsibility for Domburg.

The prisoner of war cage on Green Beach. H Houterman

CHAPTER SIX

FLUSHING – D+1

5th KOSBs clear Flushing's New Town

Brigadier McLaren wanted to push ahead before it was light and the 5th KOSBs had deployed in the streets south of 'Bexhill' overnight. Lieutenant-Colonel William Turner's men would cross the junction under cover of smoke and begin to clear the northern outskirts of the town. A Company, led by Major James Henderson, would cross first, tackling the houses lining Badhuisstraat codenamed 'Cod'. C Company would follow, under Major Thomas Kennedy-Moffat, clearing 'Grouse', the maze of streets east of Badhuisstraat. B and D Companies could then advance into the streets east of Scheldestraat code named 'Pike' and 'Partridge' and the De Schelde Shipyard beyond. Lieutenant-Colonel Turner hoped to have cleared the whole area west of the Middelburg Canal by nightfall.

The supporting artillery opened fire from across the estuary at 4:45am, shelling the buildings north of 'Bexhill'. As the 5th KOSB's waited for zero hour, disaster struck the 4th Battalion; shells were falling short onto B Company and the Carrier

5th KOSBs objectives west of the Middelburg Canal

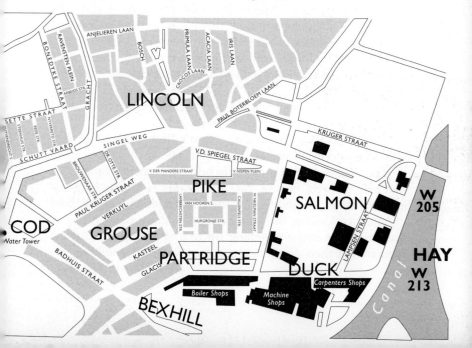

Company. Although steps were taken to extend the range of the artillery, the 4th KOSBs suffered more than a dozen casualties before the message reached the gun crews. Meanwhile, the local underground leader had paid a visit to Lieutenant-Colonel Christian Melville. He protested that shells had fallen on St Joseph's Hospital, setting the building on fire and further shelling of the area would endanger the hundreds of civilians sheltering inside. In spite of the risk, Melville sent the following uncompromising message back after conferring with his Brigade's headquarters:

Unless the Germans surrendered unconditionally, we could take no responsibility for civilian casualties.

At 5:30am Second Lieutenant Malcolm Nisbet guided A Company of the 5th KOSBs across Coosje Buskenstraat under cover of smoke. Although 'Dover's guns had fired high, accurate mortar fire targeted Major Henderson's men as they formed up along Badhuisstraat. Fourteen men were hit and in the chaos that followed, Second Lieutenant Nisbet was killed trying to rescue a wounded man. Despite the setback, Major Henderson managed to reorganise his company and before long, his men began clearing the houses along Badhuisstraat.

C Company had crossed Coosje Buskenstraat at the same time, under covering fire from 4 Commando machine-gun section. For a second time mortar shells accurately targeting the company forming up position, wounding more than a dozen men. Three officers, Major Thomas Kennedy-Moffat, the company CO, Lieutenant Eric Tullett of No 14 Platoon and Lieutenant E T Place of No 15 Platoon were among the injured. C Company's senior able officer, Lieutenant George Carmichael, reorganised the survivors leading them into 'Grouse', working east from Hobeinstraat towards Scheldestraat. Lieutenant Carmichael was later awarded the Military Cross for taking command at a critical time in the battle.

As the advance continued, Captain Robin Marshall RA, witnessed twenty Germans taking cover in a pillbox near 'Bexhill'. Realising that they could bring the junction under fire, Marshall ordered one of his gun teams forward. Sergeant Stewart Walker's men wheeled their 3.7" mountain gun behind a house overlooking the bunker and set about dismantling it. Piece by piece, some weighing up to 1/4 tonne, the gunners manhandled their equipment up the stairs, reassembling the

A 3.7″ Mountain Gun on Uncle Beach. Zeeland Library

gun in one of the bedrooms. After twenty minutes of hard work, the gun was ready and Walker gave the order to fire:

> *The first bang brought the ceiling down on us and made us look like millers. Our second round hit two Germans who had decided to leave the fort at that precise moment and they were not seen again.*

After eight shots had been fired, the outer wall of the house was in danger of collapsing and parts of the gun had gone through the floor. However, the pillbox had been destroyed; Sergeant Walker's men had, for the time being, made Bexhill a little safer.

While A and C Companies battled on, their medics set about ferrying the wounded to safety. Dover pillbox was still firing on anyone crossing Coosje Buskenstraat so the Scots resorted to using their prisoners as stretcher-bearers. Soldiers often choose their own nick-names and Bexhill was known to many as 'Hellfire Corner'.

As the 5th KOSBs fought their way though the northern outskirts of the town, the commander of the 4th KOSBs had other pressing matters to deal with. Lieutenant-Colonel Michael Melville needed to evacuate the civilians from St Joseph's Hospital before the 5th Battalion reached it. Brigadier McLaren wanted the civilians to leave via the dockyards and be taken to a safe area east of Uncle Beach. A Company of the 4th KOSBs

Civilians make their way to Uncle Beach, ready to be evacuated.
IWM BU1263

Prisoners gather on the seafront. Zeeland Library

soon found themselves overwhelmed shepherding hundreds of civilians to safety. At the same time they were forced to guard a number of Germans, eager to surrender. As the civilians made their way through the dockyard, snipers fired into the crowd from the tops of the cranes. In response, Lieutenant-Colonel Melville called forward a number of 3.7" mountain guns. Firing directly at their high targets, in what some described as a 'rook shoot', the gunners dealt with the snipers one by one.

By 11:00 am 'Grouse' was clear and B and D Companies crossed over Bexhill making for their start line. Shortly after noon Major David Haig and Major David MacDonald ordered their men across Scheldestraat to begin clearing 'Pike' and 'Partridge'. Throughout the afternoon the 5th KOSBs made slow progress, gradually clearing block after block. 'Pike' and 'Partridge' were reported clear at 2:00 pm and B and D Companies continued east into the huge machine-shops and carpenters sheds on the north side of the dock. Many Germans had withdrawn during the morning with civilians, but some remained behind determined to fight on. Under accurate mortar and machine-gun fire, the Scots winkled out the German strong points and by 5:00 pm the factory was reported to be safe.

Finally, A Company reported that 'Cod' had been cleared; it meant that the 5th KOSBs held the entire area west of the Middelburg canal. For the loss of only thirty-seven casualties, Lieutenant-Colonel Turner's men had taken all their objectives.

4 Commando's Battle for 'Dover'

While the 5th KOSBs tackled the New Town, 4 Commando still faced stiff opposition along the seafront. Commandant Phillipe Kieffer MC had taken over responsibility for the area codenamed 'Eastbourne' overnight, forming a strong cordon behind the sea front promenade with three troops. The plan was to attack at first light, clearing several strong points along the Boulevard de Ruyter.

Captain Thorburn's Troop attacked as the first streaks of grey appeared in the sky, working methodically through 'Hove', a German naval barracks. They advanced quickly and it appeared that the main garrison had fled overnight leaving behind a handful of medics to care for the wounded. A few hundred metres north, the rest of the troop entered the bombproof barracks known as 'Worthing'. They, too, found their objective

BINNENBOEZEM

GLACIS

School

Boiler Shop

De Schelde
Ship building Yard

BEXHILL

DOVER

Scherminkel ST

WAL STRAAT

Noord Straat

Kalvernier Str.

SPUI STRAAT

Korte Aelke

Rouwe Straat

Kleine Markt

W 204
WORTHING

Paarden
Markt

Slyk Straat

Molen Straat

Lange Aelke

EASTBOURNE

Bree Slop

Groote
Markt

Kerk Str.

Detailed map of the area surrounding Dover strongpoint.

Street fighting proved to be dangerous and frustrating. IWM B11634

empty except for a few wounded.

No 1 Troop's advance across Boulevard de Ruyter had alerted the Germans manning 'Dover' pillbox and its machine-guns could sweep the full length of the sea front. Heavy fire prevented Captain Thorburn's troops reaching the bombproof tower next to 'Worthing' and for the present time progress along Boulevard de Ruyter was at a standstill.

During the search that followed the commandos discovered a stash of documents and papers, including Colonel Reinhardt's intelligence log. It gave an interesting insight into the state of German morale in Flushing. One entry noted that Colonel Reinhardt issued an arrest warrant against an anti-tank platoon commander after he had withdrawn his men from their positions 'in spite of repeated official warnings that this on no account be done'. The papers also detailed unit strengths, reporting that 1019th Grenadier Regiment's companies were below half strength.

As No 1 Troop fought its way along the seafront, Commandant Kieffer had taken steps to engage 'Dover' from another direction. At 7:00 am No 5 Troop began to work its way along Coosje Buskenstraat. By breaking holes through the garden walls, a technique known as 'mouse-holing', Captain Alexandre Lofi's men advanced unseen towards 'Dover'. Progress was painfully slow, however, one section eventually stationed a PIAT team on the roof of a cinema, overlooking the strong point. As they drew closer to their objective Captain Lofi ordered No 1 Section to cross over Coosje Buskenstraat and under heavy fire his men made the suicidal run. Now it was possible for both sections to advance under cover to within assaulting distance.

However, as the commandos prepared to assault the pillbox, they were ordered to withdraw; Battalion headquarters had managed to obtain air support. From a safe distance the commandos watched in awe as the Typhoons swept in over the sea, targeting 'Dover' with their rockets and cannons.

No 5 Troop resumed its advance on 'Dover' in the afternoon taking up positions overlooking the end of Boulevard Bankert. A furious gun battle followed, and before long a group of Germans evacuated the house next to 'Dover' pillbox. Many were shot down as they ran down the street towards the Grand Hotel Britannia. No 1 Section moved forward next, taking cover

Flushing seafront, devastated during the attack on 'Dover'.

behind an anti-tank wall at the end of Coosje Buskenstraat. Although the wall had been built to stop vehicles entering the town, it now provided useful cover for the commandos' PIAT team. The final suicidal dash involved placing a 'made-up charge' against the door of the bunker:

> *Corporal Lapont volunteered to carry out this hazardous task. Just as he was about to dash forward, a white flag appeared from the embrasure, and the battle for DOVER had been won.*

Captain Lofi's men warily entered the strong point and found three officers and fifty-four men, many of them wounded.

As the prisoners were escorted from the pillbox, heavy fire along the seafront temporarily panicked the senior German officer, but as the danger passed the commandos were amused by an arrogant request:

> *The Company Commander himself, although slightly wounded and badly shaken, soon recovered the typical brand of self-assertiveness and arrogance and demanded an escort to take*

him back to DOVER for his best trousers and his service dress.
Not surprisingly, the commandos had seen and heard enough over the course of the day, to refuse the request. During the battle Captain Lofi's men had been surprised to discover a member of No 6 Troop, cut off since the previous morning. While he hid, the commando witnessed a barbaric act:

> *The Germans had re-entered this house after our troops left it, and, finding British equipment lying in it, had taken the entire family who lived there outside and shot them in cold blood.*

It had been a stern reminder that there were still fanatical elements at large in the town.

The Nolle Gap

With 'Dover' clear, No 4 Commando had secured the sea front and made 'Bexhill' crossroads safe to cross. There was, however, little time to rest. As the commandos prepared to hand over their sector to the 7/9th Royal Scots, new orders came through from Brigade. Brigadier McLaren instructed Lieutenant-Colonel Dawson to prepare to move to the northern outskirts of the town.

> *It was known that the rest of 4 Special Service Brigade was moving rapidly south along the dunes. 47 Commando was approaching Dishoek, only two miles from Flushing, but they still faced a number of coastal batteries. Brigadier Leicester wanted assistance, if 4 Commando could advance north west along the coast, they could attack the German strong points from an unexpected direction.*

The plan involved 4 Commando crossing the Nolle Gap, one of the breaches in the dike, north of the town. The gap posed many problems, huge slabs of concrete and broken beach obstacles left over from the bombing littered the gap. At low tide the channel was a torrent of fast flowing water, far too strong for the Buffaloes. It was hoped the current would subside at high tide allowing the LVTs to swim over the debris.

Lieutenant-Colonel Dawson did not receive the order to withdraw and reform until late and in the maze of ruined streets, platoon and section commanders struggled to assemble their men together. 4 Commando's report despairs over the situation:

> *It was, of course, dark long before the order to withdraw could be sent out, and there were no facilities for briefing troops, and*

no time even for the normal careful check of weapons. Eventually we had to contemplate the unpleasant prospect of priming grenades by moonlight in the LVT whilst ploughing through a rather choppy sea.

Lieutenant-Colonel Dawson was completely against the operation, acutely aware that his men were tired and hungry. He was also concerned by the shortage of small arms ammunition.

As high tide approached 4 Commando gathered in Gravestraat alongside a line of waiting Buffaloes. With trepidation the men waited for the order to mount up, while their officers worked frantically to cobble a plan together. However, at the last moment the operation was postponed; 4 Commando's report sums up the episode:

The inability of the artillery to co-operate on this occasion gave the coup-de-grace to a plan which could only have succeeded if all the Gods had been whole-heartedly with us... In this manner a remarkable and somewhat inexplicable incident was satisfactorily terminated.

Commandos study the Nolle Gap.
Zeeland Library

Troops of 4 Commando make their way along Coosje Buskenstraat
H Houterman

At long last, No 4 Commando was able to have a well-earned rest. Their speed and tenacity during the clearing of Flushing had prevented the loss of many lives, both soldiers and civilians.

The 7/9th Royal Scots attack on the Grand Hotel Britannia

As D+1 drew to a close, Lieutenant-Colonel Michael Melvill, the commanding officer of the 7/9th Royal Scots, was called into Brigadier McLaren's headquarters where he was given orders to capture the Grand Hotel Britannia on the western outskirts of the town. The hotel was suspected of housing the headquarters of the Flushing garrison and the Royal Scots were expected to attack it while 4 Commando made its way to the Noelle Gap. Even though the commando's operation was cancelled at the last minute, McLaren still wanted the German headquarters cleared.

The hotel stood on a wide embankment, forming part of the sea wall and although the position was protected by a maze of trenches and bunkers, the garrison had been estimated at no

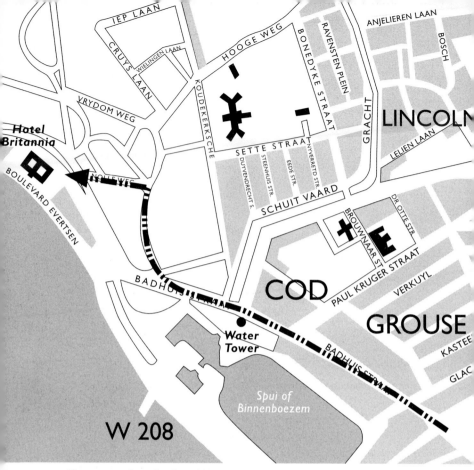

The approach to the Grand Hotel Britannia, the flooding extended as far east as the water tower.

more than fifty men. A frontal approach, along the Boulevard de Bankert, had been ruled out as too dangerous. Fortified hotels and pillboxes covered the sea front and after the experiences with 'Dover', McLaren was sure that the cornered Germans would fight to the last. The plan was to approach from the rear, in the hope of taking the garrison by surprise.

At first Lieutenant-Colonel Melvill instructed D Company, under Major Arnaud Chater, to make the attack. As a precaution, Major Hugh Rose's B Company was added later in case there were more Germans than expected. C Company, under Captain Gordon Thomson, and half the Carrier platoon, under Captain Kenneth Buchanan, also joined the assault force to provide supporting fire. It was a fortunate afterthought; the

Germans were not the only ones in for a surprise. The approach to the hotel would involve wading through floodwaters of unknown depth and Melvill arranged for 'Mae West' lifejackets. For troops who had spent months training for mountain warfare, their first battle was going to be an unforgettable experience.

At 1:45 am the Royal Scots set off through the darkened streets and as they passed warily down Badhuisstraat, fires cast an eerie glow across the town. Making their way forward, the Scots were dismayed to feel cold water splashing over the tops of their boots, the floodwater had risen far higher than expected. In front they could just make out a huge lake of sea water.

As the lead company approached a dangerous bottleneck, the bridge over the Waterweg canal, shots rang out, wounding several men. A machine-gun post stationed in the water tower overlooking the bridge barred the way forward. As men dived for cover and returned fire, others dealt with the wounded. One of the injured, CSM John Young, was in danger of being swept away by the floodwater until Private Andrews came to the rescue.

While the stretcher bearers went to work, Major Rose sent Sergeant Sandy's section forward to deal with the Germans holding the tower. They quickly stormed the water tower and before long seven prisoners were being escorted to the rear. Although one problem had been dealt with, the Royal Scots faced another danger as shells began crashing down on their

Aerial view of the seafront after the battle, the Royal Scots approached the hotel from the right. H Houterman

Hotel Britannia

positions. They appeared to be part of the supporting barrage, however, problems with the radio sets meant that there was no way of contacting the artillery. All the men could do was find cover in doorways and wait for the barrage to end but as the minutes ticked by the casualties began to mount. and by the time the shelling ceased, a large number, including over half the Carrier platoon, had been wounded.

The barrage eventually came to an end at 3:15am and leaving the Battalion MO, Captain Peter Clothier, and the padre, Rev James Wood, behind to evacuate the wounded, Melvill decided to push on. By now the water level has risen to alarming depths and before long the men were waist deep in freezing cold sea water. The men did their best to move forward, carrying their equipment above their heads, but progress was slow. Eventually the water rose up to the men's armpits, making it difficult to keep their balance. Holding arm in arm, those with heavier weapons had to be steadied by others in the chain. Occasionally a man would slip and disappear briefly beneath the water, before his comrades rescued him.

While his men edged closer to the objective, Lieutenant-Colonel Melvill established his tactical headquarters on Vrijdomweg. Soon afterwards he received a strange request from B Company; a request that nearly led to disaster:

> Major Rose asked for permission to work forward to find a shallower FUP [forming up point]. In doing so, the Battalion 'Snake' formation found themselves almost on to their objective, and 'asked for permission to assault now'. This was agreed to by Colonel Melvill and instructed that all command 'tie-up' at this point and organise the assault forward.

Rose's company had stumbled onto a pillbox covering the rear of the hotel in the darkness. With no time or space to manoeuvre, Lieutenant Joseph Cameron's Platoon attacked the bunker with 'tremendous cheers and cries of "Up the Royals"', while the Carrier Platoon gave supporting fire. Although the pillbox was taken, the rattle of machine-guns and rifles had aroused the main garrison in the hotel.

As Cameron's men took thirty-six dazed prisoners in the bunker, a number of machine-guns and four-barrelled flak cannon opened fire. The flak cannon was sited on the roof of the German headquarters and it possessed a commanding view of the area. Although many of the Royal Scots ran forward, taking

The German view of the Royal Scots approach to the hotel, the area was flooded during the attack. H Houterman

shelter at the foot of a steep embankment behind the hotel, the tail end of B Company, were caught in the open and had to fall back. They took cover in a nearby house, disturbing the German occupants. After driving off the counter-attack with his Bren gun, Corporal Chisholm led the sections across to the embankment to rejoin the rest of the company.

The Royal Scots were now in a predicament. Although they were hidden from view while they stayed at the foot of the embankment, any move forwards or backwards would bring them under fire. Pillboxes, linked by a trench covered the top of the slope, blocking the way forward. Major Rose tried to find a way to outflank the headquarters, but his search proved fruitless; snipers and machine-guns covered every approach to the hotel.

Having no other options, Major Rose and Major Chater decided to rush the back door of the hotel, in the hope of getting some men inside. After targeting a door with PIAT shells, Lieutenant Harold George led a dozen men across to the building through the gauntlet of bullets while the rest of B Company provided covering fire. After breaking through the damaged door, George's party began to explore the ground

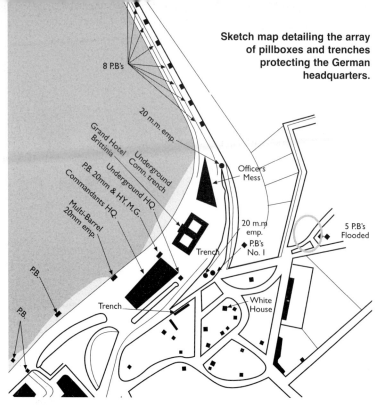

8 P.B's

20 m.m. emp.

Grand Hotel
Brittinia

Underground
Comn. trench

P.B. 20mm & H.Y.M.G.

Underground HQ.

Commandants HQ.

Multi-Barrel
20mm emp.

P.B.

P.B.

Officers
Mess

20 m.m.
emp.

P.B.'s
No. 1

Trench

20 m.m
emp.

5 P.B's
Flooded

Trench

White
House

floor of the hotel. After a nerve-racking search it became apparent that the Germans had withdrawn to the upper floors. Having established a foothold in the hotel, Major Rose decided to send more troops across to reinforce Lieutenant George. Following a pre-arranged signal, Lieutenant Cameron's platoon made the mad dash across the driveway while the rest of the Royal Scots targeted the roof of the hotel.

While the search of the hotel continued, the Germans had recovered sufficiently to make a counter-attack. As Major Rose and Major Chater waited on the embankment for news from the hotel, the Germans made several attempts to drive the Scots from their precarious position. One party established themselves in a house overlooking the embankment [labelled the White House on the map], bringing the Royal Scots under fire. Meanwhile, a determined counter-attack from the north almost overran Lieutenant John Widdowson's platoon. Even Lieutenant-Colonel Melvill's headquarters came under attack from a hidden sniper.

As he relocated his headquarters under cover of smoke,

Fire devastated the Grand Hotel Britannia. H Houterman

Melvill was rapidly coming to the conclusion that he faced far more than fifty Germans. He realised that he was greatly outnumbered and in danger of being overrun. As soon as it became light the Germans would be able to drive his men from the embankment, leaving the Hotel Britannia firmly in German hands. The Battalion war diary sums up the Royal Scots predicament:

> 20mm in such a position that it completely dominated the situation, and was not approachable. Two platoons in the hotel, which was burning furiously. Ammunition short. Enemy in considerable strength. Only communication to Bde HQ via Gunner 22 set. Casualties - appeared to be very high.

In the absence of a radio link, Melvill sent Lieutenant Joseph Brown, the intelligence officer, back to Brigade headquarters. He was to request assistance and arrange for the re-supply of ammunition. Once at Brigade HQ, McLaren made it clear to Lieutenant Brown that the Royal Scots must immediately pull back from the area around the hotel. Typhoons would be called in to deal with the flak cannon once the Scots had withdrawn. In the meantime, McLaren would arrange reinforcements for a larger attack.

However, as Lieutenant Brown returned to his Battalion headquarters, the situation at the hotel had taken a new turn. As it began to get light, Major Rose and Major Chater were increasingly concerned by the lack of contact with the men in

113

the hotel. Although shots had been heard, no one knew if Lieutenant George and Lieutenant Cameron were still active. Smoke and flames from the hotel windows indicated that the hotel was well alight and before long the building would have to be evacuated.

Captain Thomson ordered Lieutenant Beveridge's platoon forward to reinforce B Company on the embankment but he soon found his position under fire. With Major Rose's permission, Beveridge led his men across to the hotel to join the men inside. Major Chater followed in the hope of joining his men but he was killed as soon as he broke cover; Thomson was also fatally wounded as he made the dash to the hotel.

Meanwhile, C Company had completed its search of the hotel and although they had cleared the first two floors, steel reinforced doors prevented access to the roof where German snipers were still holding out. With the building ablaze and no way onto the roof the three Lieutenants, George, Cameron and Beveridge, were forced to evacuate. As they left the building, Lieutenant George spotted a machine-gun team moving its weapon onto the embankment. Realising the imminent danger, George rushed the three-man team, shooting them down with his pistol.

The Scots found themselves trapped. The flak cannon on the roof of the building next to the Grand Hotel Britannia covered the rear of the burning building, making it impossible to reach the embankment. Not to be deterred, Lieutenant Beveridge began to scale the outer wall of the building. By clinging to drainpipes and window ledges, he climbed several floors before scrambling onto the roof. The startled flak gun crew ran to safety as the officer threw himself over the parapet. It seemed that nothing could stop the determined Scots.

With the main threat to his platoon eliminated, Beveridge returned to his men and they set about clearing the pillboxes behind the hotel. As Lieutenants Beveridge and Cameron fought their way through the trenches, they stumbled on the entrance to an underground bunker. After shooting the sentry the two officers broke down the door and once inside they were astonished to find dozens of Germans seeking refuge from the fighting. They had stumbled across the main German command centre. The headquarters staff of 1019th Regiment, including its commander, *Oberst* Eugen Reinhardt, and 130 officers and men

Oberst Reinhardt considers his future in captivity

surrendered to the surprised Scots.

While the battle continued at the hotel, Lieutenant-Colonel Melvill was anxious to discover the truth about his Battalion's position. After climbing out of upper storey window and shinning down a rope, Melvill managed to escape the notice of the German snipers targeting his headquarters. As he made his way towards the hotel, Lieutenant-Colonel Melvill could see Major Rose's men pinned to the embankment. Ignoring warnings to take cover, Melvill waded forward through the receding floodwater to join his men. He was soon spotted and a burst of machine-gun fire wounded the CO and killed his signaller. Unable to move, Lieutenant-Colonel Melvill lay in the floodwater and with his cries of 'On the Royal's' ringing in their ears, the incensed Scots charged over the top of the embankment. In Major Rose's words:

> *When we saw the CO drop, we went hot with rage. Every Jock*
> *on that embankment was out to avenge him.*

Lieutenant Widdowson led the assault on the officers' mess, north of the hotel, hurling grenades into pillboxes and through windows, while C Company cleared the buildings along to the south. In the face of this furious onslaught, the Germans around the hotel soon capitulated.

With *Oberst* Reinhardt's assistance, a cease-fire was arranged and Lieutenant-Colonel Melvill watched in amazement as his men rounded up their prisoners. Six hundred dazed Germans eventually surrendered; it was rather more than the fifty men quoted in the original orders. Another fifty were found lying dead in their bunkers.

The battle had cost the Royal Scots dearly; over twenty had been killed and dozens more had been wounded. Major Hugh Rose was awarded the Distinguished Service Order for leading the battle, while Lieutenant Joe Cameron received the Military Cross for his part in clearing the hotel

CHAPTER SEVEN

BATTLE OF THE DUNES

While the battle for Flushing raged on, 4 Special Service Brigade continued its two-pronged advance along the coast of Walcheren. Brigadier Leicester's primary objective on 2 November was to push south-west through Zoutelande, heading for Flushing. The weather was making it impossible to land supplies at Westkapelle and the sooner Leicester linked up with 155 Brigade, the better.

48 Royal Marine Commando capture Zoutelande

At first light on 2 November, 48 Commando found that the Germans had abandoned their flak cannon and withdrawn from W13. Lieutenant-Colonel Moulton was anxious to renew the advance as soon as possible and he ordered A Troop, led by Captain Daniel Flunder, to pursue the Germans along the dunes towards Zoutelande.

Since first light the Canadian artillery across the estuary had been targeting A Troop's first objective, a series of pillboxes, codenamed W287. As Flunder's men approached the bunkers, five minutes of intense bombardment broke the Germans' spirit and before long the commandos had rounded up twenty shaken

Zoutelande and the high dunes to the south east, captured by 48 Commando

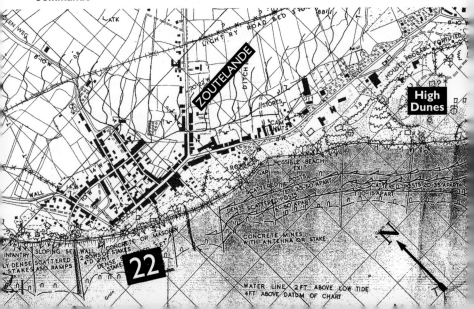

Zoutelande church, damaged by a shell from HMS *Erebus*. H Houterman

prisoners. As A Troop trudged along the dunes it seemed that the Germans were withdrawing towards Zoutelande. Occasional bursts of machine-gun fire brought the advance to a standstill from time to time but the enemy had usually fled before the marines were close enough to fire back. At one point a 'fanatical rifle-grenadier' refused to surrender and eventually had to be silenced by A Troop's Bren gun; it was a stern reminder that there was still an element of fanaticism on the island.

Captain Flunder sensed that the Germans were falling back to regroup and he was anxious to keep up the momentum of the advance. As long as his men kept moving, the Germans were unable to form a defensive position. At 11:00am A Troop reached the dunes overlooking Zoutelande, finding a series of bunkers overlooking the village. Hardly pausing to reform, Flunder ordered his men forward. They quickly negotiated the minefields covering the strong point and managed to penetrate the strong point before the Germans could react. A brisk fire-fight followed, but once the commandos had entered the bunkers the Germans capitulated. Although his men were tired, Captain Flunder was anxious to push on to capture the high dunes overlooking the village.

While Flunder was pushing his men to their limits, tension was mounting at Brigade headquarters. After the disastrous landing at Westkapelle, 47 Royal Marine Commando was finally ready to take its part in the battle. Lieutenant-Colonel Phillips accompanied Brigadier Leicester to 48 Commando's headquarters late in the morning with the intention of taking over the advance, However, they found Lieutenant-Colonel Moulton facing a dilemma. He was aware that Captain Flunder had pushed on beyond Zoutelande, but attempts to contact A Troop had so far failed. Moulton had suspicions that his subordinate had deliberately turned off his radio set to avoid being recalled. It was an unorthodox way of disobeying orders and it would be some time before Moulton regained control of the situation.

Captain Flunder eventually came back on air once his men had secured a position on the high dunes overlooking the village. With a mixture of frustration and satisfaction, Lieutenant-Colonel Moulton ordered his errant captain to halt.

In the meantime, Lieutenant-Colonel Phillips led his men south, eventually entering Zoutelande at 1:00 pm where they were met by a sea of orange flags as the local

Captain Daniel Flunder.

population turned out to meet their liberators. Although Zoutelande had been saved from prolonged bombardment, there was one last scare. As Captain Flunder assured the mayor that his village was safe, a final shell from HMS *Erebus* crashed through the church roof.

During the afternoon, Phillips' men relieved 48 Commando and continued their tiring hike south-east along the dunes.

47 Commando's view of Dishoek as it set off from Zoutelande.

Parts of the anti-tank barrier still lay hidden in the woods near Klien Valkenisse.

Early attempts to bring Weasels along the beach had been prevented by batteries along the coast and 47 Commando were forced to carry all their equipment on their backs. Meanwhile, 48 Commando withdrew to rest and while A and Y Troops gathered in Zoutelande the rest of Moulton's men returned to W13 for shelter.

48 Commando had managed to capture dozens of bunkers and hundreds of prisoners since the landing. Losses had been high; eleven officers and over eighty men had been killed or wounded since the landing. As the survivors feasted on captured rations, they had time to reflect on the difficulties they had faced over the last two days.

47 Royal Marine Commando attack W11, the Dishoek Battery

While 48 Commando rested, 47 Commando trudged along the dunes south-east of Zoutelande heading for the next major coastal battery. W11 Battery sat on the dunes high above the hamlet of Dishoek; it possessed four 150mm guns, each one protected by a huge concrete casemate.

As the commandos advanced towards Dishoek, Lieutenant-

Colonel Phillips found that he was extremely hampered by the conditions; floodwater to his left and the open beach to his right, forced him to deploy a single troop in front, while the rest snaked behind in single file.

At first, they only encountered sporadic resistance and the Germans holding the bunkers codenamed W288 quickly raise a white flag. However, a little further on, the commandos were incensed when a German turned his weapon on Lieutenant Thomson as he accepted his surrender. It was a sharp reminder of the unpredictability of the opposition. In a gully beyond Klien Valkenisse, Phillips set up his headquarters alongside an impressive tank barrier. In front lay a group of bunkers codenamed W238 and beyond, high on the dunes above Dishoek, was the formidable W11 Battery.

On the approach to the battery the dunes widened out, allowing Lieutenant-Colonel Phillips to expand his frontage. While Q Troop led the advance along the seaward side, Y Troop moved in echelon to their left. Heavy fire greeted the marines as

47 Commando's objectives.

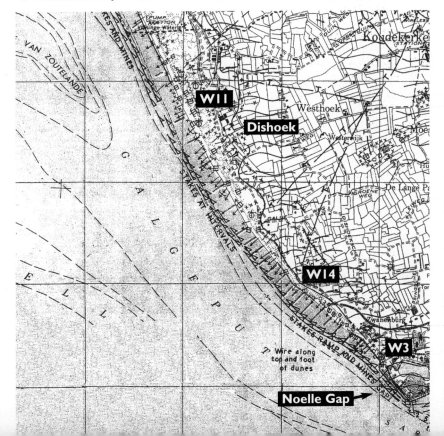

they approached W238, prompting Major Vincent to carry out a reconnaissance. Meanwhile, disaster struck his men. Mortar fire targeted Q Troop as it prepared to attack, killing and wounding more than twenty men. Captain McCormick, X Troop's leader, was also wounded as he made his way forward to assist. Captain John Forfar, 47 Commando's medical officer, eventually found the seriously injured Vincent out in front and as stretcher bearers came up to help they came under fire, (Forfar received the Military Cross for his part in the Walcheren Operation). Typhoons managed to suppress the bunkers, but with few officers left, Sergeant Esher took the lead. The survivors were relieved to find W238 abandoned; the Germans had fled along the dunes.

It was late afternoon by the time 47 Commando closed on their main objective, W11. The casemates had been targeted many times in the hope of silencing its guns, first by the RAF and then by the Naval Bombardment Squadron, (a later survey counted 148 bomb craters alone in the immediate vicinity of the battery). However, the guns had remained undamaged and continued to shell Green Beach.

By now, air support had been exhausted and all Lieutenant-Colonel Phillips could call upon was artillery support from across the estuary. Assembling far closer to the target area than considered safe, 47 Commando waited for the barrage to begin. The first objective was a searchlight position on top of a high dune and a shallow gully had to be crossed before the commandos could assault the main battery. 47 Commando had lost most of its mortars and machine-guns during the landing and Phillip's men were at a distinct disadvantage without their support weapons.

The plan was for Y Troop to assault the searchlight position while B Troop cleared the bunkers on the inland side of the dunes. The first Allied shells began to fall at 4:55 pm and in the words of the Forward Observation Officer, the fire plan looked impressive:

> [the dike] *was given by four stonks which, joined together, made a straight line running along the top of the dunes up to and including the objective.*

Five minutes later the commandos charged across the sand in a race against time. Machine-guns and mortars hidden in the houses of Dishoek hamlet immediately targeted B Troop and

One of huge casemates at the Dishoek Battery.

many were wounded, including Captain Moyes. Y Troop
suffered many casualties as it approached the searchlight and
Captain Flower was hit several times leading the final charge. A
Troop pushed on into the gully, coming under fire from the
bunkers on the dunes ahead. The attack was nothing short of
suicidal without heavy support weapons but the commandos
persisted, fighting a running battle among the bunkers.
Sergeant-Major England captured one machine-gun post, firing
his Bren gun from the hip to silence the crew. It was one of the
few successes of the afternoon.

A Troop edged forward and in the failing light, managed to
enter the battery position. Working forward, the commandos
systematically cleared the casemates, taking a number of
prisoners along the way. Eventually, the lead troop was able to
report that the battery was clear; it had taken five hours to clear
the Dishoek Battery. However, Lieutenant-Colonel Phillips'
troubles were far from over. 47 Commando had suffered heavy
casualties, in particular among its leaders; five troop leaders and
a number of other officers and senior NCO's had been
wounded, sixty commandos had also been killed or wounded.

Captain Spencer, the adjutant, and Captain Gower, the
intelligence officer, went forward to assess the situation and

they found that the commandos were far too disorganised to set up an effective defensive line. If the Germans counter-attacked at first light they could easily be overrun and the gully could easily become a death-trap if the Germans had mortars to hand. Lieutenant-Colonel Phillips faced no alternative, he ordered his men to withdraw to the searchlight position to regroup. As Captain Spencer organised the new defensive position the stretcher bearers were kept busy searching the dunes for wounded.

While 47 Commando consolidated its new line, Brigadier Leicester paid a visit to their headquarters. Anxious to speed up the capitulation of W11, he urged Phillips's to reoccupy the battery while it was still dark. Leicester received a flat refusal; 47 Commando could do no more at the present time.

Even though they had been beaten once, the Germans were determined to retake their position. *Oberleutnant* Helmut Lange reorganised his men and in the early hours, they launched a determined counter-attack, and for a time 47 Commando was in danger of being overrun. In the words of the Brigade diary, the commando was 'very thin on the ground'. Sensing the commandos' weakness, the Germans called out for their surrender:

> *A firm negative was substantiated by determined offensive action, and what might have been an unpleasant situation was saved.*

The following morning the weather took a turn for the worse and gale force winds lashed the beaches as 47 Commando prepared to renew the assault on the battery. Captain Flunder arrived at Lieutenant-Colonel Phillips headquarters and, after receiving a frosty welcome following his exploits at Zoutelande, took his men forward to establish a fire position. As A Troop moved inland, German positions on the dunes came alive, targeting Flunder's men. Running forward the commandos took cover in an unguarded pumping station from where they could return fire.

While Captain Flunder's men gave covering fire, 47 Royal Marine Commando launched their attack on W11. A Troop were quickly pinned down by heavy fire as they attempted to cross the gully. With the attack at a standstill, X Troop crawled along the beach while A Troop engaged the machine-gun posts high on the dunes. Once X Troop had outflanked the main line of resistance, Captain Spencer's men charged up the dunes entering the complex of casemates. Meanwhile, A Troop took advantage of the distraction advancing forward from the gully. Facing attacks from two directions, the Germans capitulated and, as the German officers began to call their men out of their shelters, the commandos grimly counted dozens of German bodies strewn throughout the bunkers.

It had been a bloody battle but before the last of the prisoners had been rounded up, Lieutenant-Colonel Phillips was taking steps to press on. He wanted to clear the last stretch of dunes before the Germans had time to regroup and while troops remained behind to mop up the battery, the rest headed south. The tired commandos cursed the weather as they trudged along the dunes; rain lashed the beaches as high winds whipped sand into their faces. Ahead lay the final active battery before Flushing, W4.

Although the battery had been isolated by the floods and enemy action for several days, *Kapitan* Köll, was determined to put up a show of resistance and as the marines moved closer a scattering of shots caused casualties. Although it appeared that 47 Commando had a fight on its hands, a white flag appeared above the strong point as they prepared to attack. At first Lieutenant-Colonel Phillips sent Captain Spencer and his interpreter, Lieutenant Winter to negotiate with Köll. However, on their return the two officers found their leader in an uncompromising mood. Köll's demands for an honourable capitulation were to be denied; Phillips wanted an unconditional surrender. Spencer and Winter delivered the demands but on their return, shots rang out from the bunkers. It appeared that the commandos would have to make one final charge. As they nervously waited

Korvettenkapitän **Hans Köll.**

for the order to attack, they were relieved to see Germans emerging from the bunkers in front, hands held high. As 47 Commando looked on, they watched in amazement as 200 men filed out. Soon afterwards Phillips' met Köll:

> ... *handing me his Luger pistol,* [Köll] *said. 'You must shoot me if you think I have not done my duty.' I was so relieved and delighted that I could have embraced him.*

Had Phillips known he had been outnumbered so heavily, the outcome could have been tragically different.

By 2:30 on 3 November all resistance between Westkapelle and Flushing had come to an end; it was not, however, the end of the battle for the island by far. As the young marines trudged north along the dunes with their prisoners, they had time to survey the scenes of devastation. An officer of 4 Commando made the same trek the following day and recorded what he saw:

> On the left of the track the dunes, shifting sand, rose to heights of one hundred feet or more. There were shelters and pillboxes everywhere, all with an indescribable litter of German equipment, food, clothing and personal effects, especially letters, strewn about them. The track itself was narrow, the marching column had to move in single file, and pitted with huge bomb craters. On the right of the track lay the floodwaters stretching away inland as far as the eye could see in a smooth sheet, broken here and there by the upper storeys of houses or tree tops. No words or photographs can adequately convey the utter desolation of the scene and, looking across the island from the sand dunes, it was easy enough to understand the despair which must have gripped the German garrison when this catastrophe was unleashed on them.

The Battle for Domburg

We had left 41 Royal Marine Commando engaged in the ruins of Domburg. However, Brigadier Leicester wanted Palmer's men to assist in the drive south towards Flushing. 10 (Inter-Allied) Commando eventually reached the town at 4:00 on D+1 and before dark had managed to take over responsibility for the town. Lieutenant-Colonel Peter Laycock was, however, concerned by his exposed position:

> Only half the town had been captured and there was much sniping and machine-gun fire going on, on arrival.

Laycock's force was smaller than 41 Commando (the two French Troops were engaged in Flushing and the Dutch Troop had been split, its men acting as interpreters with the local population) so as a compromise, Palmer agreed to leave two troops in support. As Lieutenant Pierre Roman took out the first fighting patrol to 'get the lie of the land', Laycock was pleased to welcome three Buffaloes laden with ammunition and food.

A Churchill AVRE tank moves cautiously through Domburg. Zeeland Library

Meanwhile, Leicester had not been idle. Recognising Laycock's need for assistance he had ordered the remaining handful of tanks to Domburg, (three had been 'drowned' overnight by the rising tide around Westkapelle). Although their journey along the flooded road was arduous, with the help of engineers, they eventually got through. 10 Commando's delight is echoed in their war diary:

> *Outlook considerably brightened by arrival of Major Pocock, commanding squadron of 1st Lothians, who brought up the relics of the squadron, two Shermans and two AVREs.*

The presence of armour considerably strengthened Laycock's hold on Domburg, and many Germans withdrew to a safe distance. Overnight, Laycock's men were kept busy escorting refugees to safer areas while the Germans continued to mortar the ruins. Despite the dangers, several locals tried to return to their homes and the commandos had considerable difficulty keeping some out of German-held areas.

The following day, 10 Commando began in earnest to clear the village. Under direction of the commandos, Major Duncan Pocock's tanks moved through the streets, systematically destroying suspected strong points and, in the face of armour, German resistance faded as many withdrew into the woods to the east. A large water tower on the sea front, used as an observation point, was one such target. A few rounds from the two Shermans brought resistance to an end and before long the occupants came running out, in fear for their lives.

Meanwhile, plans to advance east were underway. It was hoped that No 5, the Norwegian Troop, could make progress along the dunes while No 4, the Belgian Troop, entered the woods east of the village.

A rolling barrage from the Canadian guns south of the estuary preceded the attack and even though a 1,000-yard safety margin had been allowed, some shells still fell short. With support from two tanks, the Norwegians advanced along the dunes, encountering minefields, protected by high wire fences. Ladders were used to enter the strong points and Captain Rolv Hauge, the troop commander, was wounded in the arm climbing one fence. Although the Norwegians encountered sporadic fire, (killing one man and wounding their sergeant-major), they managed to get close to the German positions. Lieutenant Olav Gausland eventually brought all resistance to an end by throwing a well-placed hand grenade through the entrance. Dozens of prisoners emerged moments later, hands held high above their heads.

Despite his wound, Captain Hauge had remained in command of the Norwegian Troop, regrouping it before pushing on along the dunes towards W18. Although they encountered several more entrenched positions, the Norwegians attacked relentlessly, each time taking large numbers of prisoners. Hauge eventually reported to the medical officer once his men had secured a defensive perimeter. He was immediately sent back for medical aid and eventually evacuated across the estuary. His leadership was later rewarded with the Military Cross.

Meanwhile, the Belgian Troop moved cautiously into the woods east of Domburg, with support from two of Pocock's tanks. Although few Germans were seen, snipers and mortar shells managed to wound a number of men. The Belgians noticed how the German artillery crews preferred to keep their distance rather than engage the commandos. In the words of the battalion diarist, 'the Kriegsmarine did not like close fighting'.

Although outnumbered, with determination and skill Laycock's men had managed to advance over half a mile through difficult country, taking over 200 Germans prisoner.

CHAPTER EIGHT

CLEARING FLUSHING

3 November, was a day of consolidation and preparation for Brigadier McLaren. He was determined to secure his perimeter before sending troops into the outlying areas of the town. A Company of the 7/9th Royal Scots finally cleared the spit of land, code named 'Falmouth', east of the landing beach where Germans had held out for two days. B and D Companies of the 5th KOSBs continued to clear the De Schelde Aircraft factory throughout the day, hunting out a few determined fanatics. Many times the Scots called for the Germans to surrender but more often than not, they were compelled to take each pillbox or foxhole by force. Accurate machine-gun and mortar fire directed

Flushing Docks, captured by the 5th KOSBs on 4 November.

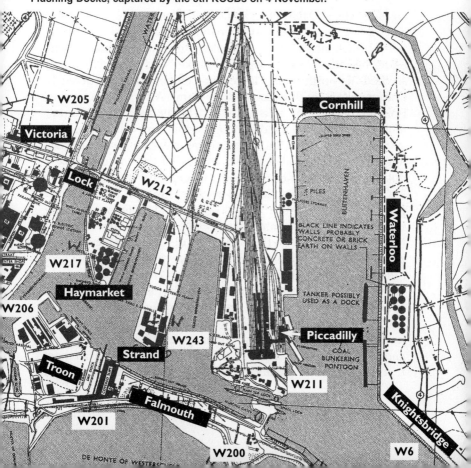

from the oil refinery, codenamed 'Haymarket' across the canal, continued to harass the Scots but they were powerless to react with own weapons. An artillery shoot carried out by guns across the estuary targeted the area in the afternoon and a Typhoon strike on 'Haymarket' and 'Strand', boosted the Scots' morale. They watched in awe while the planes swooped in low to unleash their rockets, before pulling up at the last moment in a steep climb.

Although the day had been relatively quiet, Brigadier McLaren had been studying how to clear the final German held area, Flushing Docks. The only access was across lock gates on the Middelburg Canal and McLaren knew that they were set for demolition. If the 5th KOSBs could rush the gates under cover of darkness, the lead sections might be able to overpower the German engineers before they could set off the charges. It was a risk that McLaren was prepared to take.

At 2:30am on 4 November, B Company dashed across the lock gates under cover of smoke, surprising the Germans on the far side. Major David Haig's men had managed to capture the gates intact, leaving the way open into Flushing Docks. Heading north Haig's men secured a line along the railway embankment under heavy fire, bypassing 'Haymarket' and 'Strand'. Having secured his north flank Lieutenant-Colonel Turner, ordered D Company across the canal at 3:45am. After overpowering isolated pockets of resistance in 'Haymarket' and 'Strand', Major David MacDonald's men headed for Flushing railway station, codenamed 'Picadilly'. After clearing two pillboxes north of the station, D Company rounded the end of the next dock basin, codenamed 'Cornhill', meeting stiff opposition.

C Company was following in close support, and the lead platoon headed south into 'Waterloo'. Lieutenant George Carmichael's men immediately came under fire from a troublesome pillbox on the dockside and for a time the advance came to a halt. Unable to outflank the position, Carmichael called up the platoon PIAT team and a couple rounds from Private John Finlay's weapon soon drove the Germans into the open. A few bursts from Company Sergeant Major Andrew Lees' Bren gun made sure they did not get far. With the way forward clear, C Company continued south through 'Waterloo' and 'Knightsbridge' and at 8:10am Lieutenant Carmichael reported that all of the dockyards east of the Middelburg Canal

The 5th KOSBs rounded up dozens of prisoners in Flushing dockyards
IWM BU1245

were clear. For a second time Lieutenant-Colonel Turner had reason to be proud of his men; for the loss of over twenty casualties, his men had taken over one hundred prisoners and completed the liberation of Flushing.

The Middelburg Canal

Despite a full morning's work, the day was far from over for B Company. Brigadier McLaren wanted the 5th KOSBs to follow up their success by probing north along the canal towards Middelburg. The approach along the canal was an ordeal in itself; at high tide floodwater came right up to the canal banks, restricting the Scots front to a few metres. Major Haig's men tentatively made their way along the canal and although

The Middelburg Canal, surrounded by floodwaters.

progress was painfully slow, the slender column advanced without incident.

At 4:00 pm the head of the column was only a mile and half from Middelburg when disaster struck. The leading patrol detonated a mine, injuring the battalion intelligence officer, Lieutenant Peter Grant, and a corporal. The blast alerted the enemy dug into the opposite embankment, and moments later B Company came under fire. With nightfall approaching, Lieutenant-Colonel Turner ordered his men to pull back from the exposed position. There was little more he could do; both banks of the canal would have to be cleared simultaneously if the advance was to continue.

The 4th KOSBs took over the Middelburg canal overnight and the plan was for Lieutenant-Colonel Melvill to renew the advance at first light. While D Company, under Major George Harcourt Rae, probed along the west bank of the canal, Major Colin Hogg led B Company along the towpath on the opposite bank. Orders from above reminded Melvill's men to encourage Germans to give themselves up, if the opportunity presented itself: 'Appreciate that enemy is ripe for surrender – close lookout to be kept for white flags, which should be strictly respected.'

As the two companies made their way north through the 5th Battalion's positions, they were pleased to see two artillery shoots and a Typhoon rocket strike on suspected strong points. At 9:15 am, B Company sprang the German trap, coming under heavy fire from several directions. Snipers targeted the lead men, while machine-gun fire from the opposite bank of the canal raked the column. As Major Hogg's men went to ground, accurate mortar fire added to their misery. The battalion diary describes B Company's dilemma:

> Little chance of cover - axis of advance narrow footpath with bad flooding on the right; railway on the left probably mined; embankment on other side of railway definitely occupied.

Although his company had only sustained four casualties, Hogg realised his position was hopeless and withdrew his men to safer positions.

D Company advanced up the west bank of the canal to assist their comrades and as the head of the column drew level with B Company, three Germans surrendered. Lieutenant Lars Gjendemsö interrogated the men on the spot and quickly established the reason why their comrades would fight on:

> There was a pillbox on the embankment, midway between B Company and the canal bend. This was manned by about thirty strong and commanded by a Major whose order had been 'No Surrender'.

The approach along the Middelburg Canal was fraught with danger, note 52nd Division's insignia on the flag. H Houterman

The 'Mad Major' was determined to hold out to the last.

D Company faced further problems when they stumbled on a minefield, killing one of their men. The engineers were faced with Teller mines and Schü-mines rigged with booby-trap devices; from now on, D Company's advance would be reduced to a snail's pace. As the KOSBs crept forward, an air strike by Typhoons failed to target the slit trenches and foxholes. Major Hogg withdrew to a house on the canal bank and from the upstairs windows he could see the German positions; two bunkers, surrounded by a 'warren of foxholes'. It would take substantial reserves to crack the strong point. With B Company effectively pinned down and D Company probing the minefield, the 4th KOSBs were at a standstill.

At the operations meeting that night, Lieutenant-Colonel Melville proposed to take the 'Mad Major's' bunker by surprise. B Company would send a night patrol along the narrow path to engage the strong point with PIAT rockets. There were strong objections to the suggestion and later that night the plan was cancelled; B Company would sit tight. It appeared that Brigade had plans to reach Middelburg from another direction.

Throughout the following day D Company edged slowly forward, accepting the surrender of forty-eight prisoners. B Company also collected a handful of Germans eager to give themselves up on the east bank. Meanwhile, their fanatical leader continued to fire on the Scots at every opportunity; the 'Mad Major' intended to fight on to the end.

CHAPTER NINE

DASH TO MIDDLEBURG

While the 4th KOSB made slow progress along the canal towards Middelburg, Brigadier McLaren faced a dilemma. An assault on the town, a difficult operation in view of the floodwaters, would result in high casualties amongst the civilian population. However, a long drawn out siege could lead to an equally high mortality rate. Large parts of Middelburg remained above water and thousands of people had moved in with friends and relations to escape the floods. By the beginning of November the population had virtually doubled and conditions in the town were deteriorating fast. Fresh water and food supplies were coming to an end and sanitation was becoming an issue as the influx of people put the sewerage system under severe strain. Middelburg was on the verge of an epidemic.

The population was trapped in an ever-tightening cordon as first Flushing and then the villages along the coast were liberated. Meanwhile, the 2nd Canadian Division was approaching from the east, advancing along the South Beveland isthmus. As the cordon around Middelburg tightened, tension mounted as everyone speculated what the trapped Germans would do.

Brigadier McLaren and his commanding officer, Major-General Hakewill Smith, estimated that there were about 2,000 Germans in Middelburg; the commander of the island, General Daser, was also known to be in the town. Over the past two days several local people had escaped the town and braved the floods to contact the British forces on the coast. Cornelis Antheunisse and Pieter de Kam, of the Dutch Resistance organisation *Ordedienst,* made the first attempt, rowing across to Domburg on 3 November. Three attempts were made the following night. Middelburg surgeon Everard Nauta made his way by canoe to Zoutelande, reporting to 47 Commando south of the village. Koudekerke solicitor Marinus Terwoert also reached Zoutelande by boat, accompanied by four rowers. Meanwhile, Flushing policeman Jacob van Holst made the most

Middelburg at the end of October 1944.

influential visit to 155 Brigade's headquarters in Flushing. He was convinced that General Daser might surrender under the right conditions. If 155 Brigade could reach the town with tanks, the General would be able to capitulate honourably, after all he had no armour of his own.

On the afternoon of the 5th a reconnaissance party set out towards Koudekerke, after repeated attempts to make signal contact with the town had failed. Lieutenant Joesph Brown, the Royal Scots' intelligence officer and Captain Walwin Jones, the Brigade Liaison Officer had two objectives. The first was to try and make contact with German outposts near Middelburg, in the hope of starting negotiations for surrender. The alternative, and more likely option, was to reconnoitre the far side of the town:

> To determine whether it is possible to land a battalion (transported in Water Buffaloes) to the North Road leading into Middelburg.

Progress was extremely slow across the flooded fields and great care had to be taken to avoid underwater obstacles, any of which could be booby-trapped with anti-landing charges. The suspense was lifted momentarily in Koudekerke when the Dutch mobbed Brown's Buffalo, while others shouted greetings from upper storey windows and rooftops. Although they assured them that there were no Germans outside Middelburg, the recce party turned back before it reached the town. Captain Jones decided it was unwise to continue in the failing light. He was becoming increasingly concerned by the lack of contact with brigade headquarters on the radio.

The return journey in the dark was fraught with danger and the Buffalo eventually grounded on a flooded bridge. For twelve hours Captain Jones and Lieutenant Brown waded across the flooded fields to report back and early on the 6th Brigadier McLaren welcomed the two sodden officers into his headquarters. He was interested to hear how far the Buffalo had travelled without encountering any resistance. Jones summed up that an operation was

> ... not practicable by night; but, with time and good navigation by day, it would indeed be possible, but, a percentage of casualties must be expected owing to mined areas.

Initially Brigadier McLaren intended to transport all of the 7/9th Royal Scots to the far side of the city, however, the 11th

Royal Tank Regiment could only muster twelve Buffaloes, enough for a single company. Even so McLaren was prepared to try and reach Middelburg before nightfall. At 11:00am, Major John Dawson, the Royal Scots acting CO, briefed Major Hugh Johnston, A Company's:

> *You will advance from here, across the airport along the road south of KOUDEKERKE and then proceed along the road to MIDDELBURG. It is believed that the Germans wish to surrender. You will therefore send in a party in a LVT under a Flag of Truce to demand the surrender of the city. Be careful around TER HOOGE as there may be Germans there who intend to fight.*

Johnston would be reinforced by machine-gun platoon of the Manchesters, bringing his small force to 120 men mounted in a dozen personnel carriers; hardly a strong armoured force. A Norwegian RE officer, Lieutenant Johan Goldfarb, would

The Royal Scots route to Middelburg.

Crowds gather round a Buffalo, the first sign that liberation was imminent. H Houterman

accompany Johnston to act as his interpreter, in case the opportunity to parley arose.

At 12:30pm Lieutenant Vernon Lowe drove his Buffalo out onto the flooded airfield at the head of the column. He was accompanied by a willing civilian acting as a guide across the flooded landscape. At first progress was slow and the Scots were forced to cut a way through a network of poles and wires installed to prevent gliders landing on the airstrip! Once at the far edge of the airfield, the crews floated their Buffaloes across a heavily mined anti-tank ditch with baited breath.

As the convoy edged forward Major Johnston was pleased to see a white flag above Koudekerke church tower and as they entered the village 'wild scenes of welcome' greeted the Royal Scots. Everyone was eager to help their liberators and the Buffalo drivers were quickly guided onto the Middelburg road. As the Buffaloes moved off line ahead towards Ter Hoge, Johnston called up Typhoons to cover the next stage of the advance.

Pushing on as fast as possible, the column reached Ter Hooge Chateau at 3:00 pm. The chateau had been an important headquarters during the occupation of the island and Johnston

Soldiers and civilians watch the prisoners gather, note the underground member armed with a pistol. H Houterman

was concerned that there might be active bunkers in the area. As the Buffaloes moved forward Johnston ordered Sergeant Edward Milton's and Corporal Cooper's Buffaloes to search the woods south of the road. Minutes later they came under fire from a hidden machine-gun and Johnston ordered Lance-Corporal David Sykes to drive across to assist. However, before Sykes had travelled twenty metres from the road, disaster struck. The Buffalo detonated a mine mortally wounding several men including the driver.

While the casualties were cared for in a nearby house, Johnston called back his Buffaloes ready to resume the journey into Middelburg. He could not afford to be distracted by a solitary machine-gun. A civilian joined the column, giving directions as the Buffaloes approached the edge of the town.

Lieutenant Lowe's Buffalo entered the town first, unsure of what to expect but after a brief reconnaissance Johnston was relieved to hear there had been no opposition. In fact Lieutenant Lowe had so far only encountered civilians, delighted at the prospect of being liberated. The remaining Buffaloes, seven in total, quickly followed making a tremendous racket as they climbed out of the water onto the cobbles. Roaring through the streets the Buffaloes entered the main square, taking up positions to cover all the exits. They were met by dozens of Germans intent on surrender and while Johnston organised the growing body of prisoners, Captain Jones and Lieutenant Goldfarb set off in search of the German headquarters.

As Major Johnston took stock of the situation, the number of people congregating outside the town hall was growing to alarming numbers. He knew that there were over 2,000 Germans in the town and it seemed as though they were all congregating in the main square. With no immediate hope of reinforcements, Johnston approached the local Underground Leader for assistance. Eighty men were quickly found and after being armed with German rifles, they took their place alongside the Royal Scots. Proudly sporting orange armbands, the Dutch Resistance helped to intimidate the prisoners and calm the locals gathering to watch the spectacle.

Meanwhile, Captain Jones' Buffalo was met with surprise when it pulled up outside the German headquarters in a nearby

A Buffalo parks outside the German headquarters.

square. 70th Infantry Division's staff had been based in two offices in Damplien ever since the flooding had forced them to abandon Ter Hooge. The two officers were quickly granted a meeting with General Daser but once inside Jones found the general to be uncompromising. As he explained the terms of surrender with the help of Goldfarb's translation, Daser willingly handed over his pistol. However, he refused point blank to capitulate to Jones on a matter of principle.

He regarded it as not the done thing to surrender to an officer junior to himself.

Thinking on his feet, Jones informed Daser that his staff colonel (actually Major Johnston) was on his way to complete the formal surrender and, in the meantime, he could set proceedings under way. Again Daser refused to co-operate.

With the situation outside the town hall under control, Major Johnston made his way to General Daser's headquarters accompanied by Major Thomas Newton-Dunn, the Buffalo's commanding officer. As three Buffaloes parked outside the headquarters ready to transport the prisoners to safety, Johnston was aware that the general expected to meet a full staff colonel.

A young soldier keeps watch over the gathering crowd of prisoners.
H Houterman

He did not want to disappoint the German staff officers and borrowed the 'pips' from his subaltern's tunic to look the part:

In view of the heavy preponderance of field-grey in that square, the time seemed right for some accelerated promotion.

Johnston found General Daser in a surly mood and he paced back and forth in front of his staff officers as Lieutenant Goldfarb translated the conditions of surrender. Daser eventually relented, having stipulated two conditions. The first requirement was simple to comply with, the General wanted to surrender in private to avoid humiliating in front of the people of Middelburg. The second condition was rather more unusual. Although

Major Johnston leads General Daser into captivity.

Prisoners gather in Damplein. Zeeland Library

Daser would help the Royal Scots round up the remaining Germans in the town, there was one individual he did not wish to approach. The officer in command of strong points on the canal south of the town had severed contact with headquarters several days ago. According to Daser, the officer was a determined fanatic who would not hear of surrender. It was the same 'Mad Major' that had pinned the 4th KOSBs down for the past two days.

While Johnston negotiated with the German staff, Major Newton-Dunn began a tour of the billets in the town accompanied by a senior German officer. Although many Germans had gathered in the two squares, hundreds still remained unaware of the imminent surrender; others would only surrender to a member of the Royal Scots, fearful of the crowds of Dutch gathering in the streets.

Meanwhile, in Damplien hundreds of German soldiers watched as General Daser emerged from his headquarters and escorted to a waiting Buffalo by Sergeant Grayson and two drivers. Major Johnston was anxious not to arouse the General's suspicions but at the critical moment shots were fired from across the square. Rushing across to investigate, Johnston found that two of his men had shot a prisoner as he pulled a grenade from his pocket. All he could do was order the two soldiers to strengthen the guard on General Daser.

During the commotion Major Newton-Dunn entered the square having completed his circuit of the billets. By now the German staff officer accompanying Newton-Dunn had realised how weak the British forces were and as the Buffalo pulled up alongside General Daser, he tried to raise the alarm. While the British soldiers looked on in bewilderment, Lieutenant Goldfarb immediately understood what the staff officer's intentions were. A short scuffle followed and the enlightened officer's protests were quickly stifled. Before General Daser realised he had been tricked, the troublemaker was locked in a cellar.

With the situation under control, Major Johnston established a headquarters in the Burgomaster's house and radioed for assistance. Although Brigade promised to send help as soon as possible, the 'Mad Major' blocked the shortest route from the south. In the meantime, the Royal Scots would have to sit tight and wait. The 5th Highland Light Infantry, were known to be approaching from Nieuwland to the south-east and Lieutenant

Soldiers keep watch as the local population turn out to greet their liberators.

Lowe, with a party of resistance men as guides, was sent to find them.

One thing Johnston was not short of was advice, either from the Underground or town dignitaries and he quickly established that many of the bridges into the town had been prepared for demolition. Under guard, General Daser's chief staff officer, 'a typical Nazi called Major von Kleist', led the German engineers to make the bridges safe. Although the fact is not mentioned in the war diaries, some sources say that Major Karl von Kleist was made to stand on each bridge as his men disabled the charges as an insurance against shoddy work!

While the Royal Scots waited for reinforcements Johnston asked Major Newton-Dunn to 'put on a show' to calm the mood of the captured Germans and throughout the night the Buffalo drivers drove around the streets, keeping up the pretence that there were many in the town. Meanwhile, the thousands of Dutch locals milling around the streets were becoming a cause for concern. Although many celebrating the liberation peacefully, a few went hunting for hidden parties of Germans. Sporadic firefights around the town added to the tension and according to Johnston:

> It needed only one of them to fire into that mob in the square to precipitate a stampede that would have ended in a massacre of German prisoners and the swamping of the Royal Scots picquets.

The German prisoners were becoming increasingly nervous and although they sang the *Horst Wessel* in a show of camaraderie, the onset of rain only exacerbated the situation. With so few guards Johnston could not afford to let them under cover and instead ordered the German cooks to make bread to appease the prisoners.

Around 3:00 am on 7 November, Major Johnston was relieved to welcome Lieutenant-Colonel 'Rhoddy' Rose, commanding officer of the 5th Highland Light Infantry, into his headquarters. They had been met by Lieutenant Lowe south-east of the town, and guided in by the Dutch resistance. It had been eleven hours since the Royal Scots had entered the town facing odds of twenty to one. As Captain John Arnold, GSO3 of the 52nd Division, prepared to interrogate the German officers more reinforcements arrived. Brigadier McLaren had taken steps to send as many men as possible from the south. Captain Roger Kirk led the rest of the 11th Royal Tank Regiment Buffaloes, sixteen in number, into the town carrying the 4th KOSBs. Major Johnston was also pleased to see Major John Charteris with C Company of the Royal Scots.

As the new arrivals took over responsibility for guarding the prisoners (the tally eventually came to 2,070), Major Johnston kept one man captive to the Royal Scots: General Daser;

> I felt he was ours, and that Royal Scots should continue to guard the first General we had captured.

As the Buffaloes took the Germans to Flushing and into captivity, General Daser must have reflected on the deception that had lead to his defeat. Major Johnston's combination of boldness and good fortune had prevented the loss of hundreds of lives. One wrong move and it could have all been so different for Middelburg.

CHAPTER TEN

THE FINAL BATTLE

Around noon on 4 November 41 Royal Marine Commando arrived in Domburg, after their fruitless trek south. Although they had just spent two days on the march, B Troop was sent forward to assist 10 (Inter-Allied) Commando. They would attack W18, an anti-aircraft position with a commanding position on the dunes, while the Belgian Troop advanced through the woods inland. After several hours waiting for confirmation of air support, the advance began at 3:00, after three Typhoons 'put in a brief and rather useless appearance, late'. Even so, Captain Georges Danloy's men pushed forward through the woods, hampered by snipers and mines. A number of men were wounded including Adjutant Comte Guy d'Oultremont. After advancing 800 metres and taking over one hundred prisoners, the Belgians were ordered to halt. 41 Commando's troop had run into difficulties on the approach to W18. Enfilade fire from the woods surrounding Westhove Castle (a chateau-style building) had forced Lieutenant-Colonel

Domburg and the area cleared by 10 (Inter-Allied) Commando.

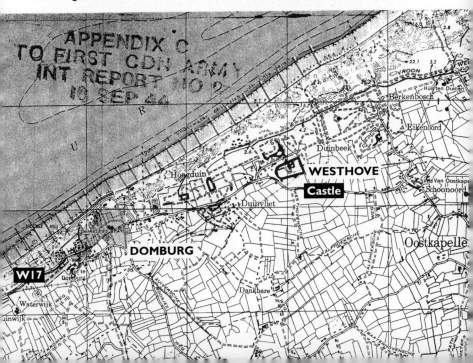

10 Commando in the woods east of Domburg. Zeeland Library

Palmer to withdraw from the exposed dunes. 10 Commando would have to clear the area before his men could reach the battery.

While some of the men spent another miserable night on the dunes, others were rather more fortunate. 41 Commando took over the inauspiciously named *'Badhotel'* (Bath Hotel), a German officer's billet, and made full use of the abandoned facilities.

The Norwegian Troop took over responsibility for 10 Commando's front overnight and prepared to renew the advance. However, appalling weather conditions meant that they would have to continue without the benefits of air support. Throughout the day patrols fought a frustrating game of hide and seek with German snipers while the engineers probed for mines and booby-traps.

During the afternoon Palmer was prepared to renew the attack on W18 and at 3:00 his men began moving cautiously along the dunes, supported by two of Major Pollock's tanks. Small arms fire and mortar fire targeted the commandos as they crept forward, and while A Troop cleared the landward side of the dunes, Y Troop, approached the battery position. A Nebelwerfer rocket launcher was quickly silenced when a lucky shot from one of the tanks destroyed its ammunition dump. As Y Troop negotiated the minefield protecting W18, one tank struck a mine, and the other withdrew to safety. Captain Peter Haydon's men would have to attack alone. Bunker after bunker surrendered as the commandos worked their way forward through the complex. Although casualties were light, Captain Peter Haydon DSO and his batman Marine Byron Moses, had been fatally wounded leading the attack. As the light began to fade the last pocket of resistance surrendered and 300 men were on their way to captivity.

While 41 Commando and 10 Commando continued to probe forward on 6 November, the two commanding officers were increasingly concerned by the shortage of supplies. Although stocks of German foodstuffs sustained the men, they were unable to fight without ammunition. The engineers had worked hard to clear the flooded coast road, but minefields eventually forced them to find another route. It would be some time before they opened a route to Domburg.

Brigadier Leicester visited 41 Commando's headquarters during the afternoon, anxious to renew the advance. However, Lieutenant-Colonel Palmer convinced him of the need to build up supplies. While the commandos waited they watched as Typhoons strafed targets along the coast. The three remaining tanks spent the afternoon searching for targets around the Black Hut position:

> ... a number of pillboxes and OP's [Observation Posts] in the dunes to the north were shot up and further rounds put into the Black Hut area and the large concrete emplacement. A wooden screen had been put across the slit but this was soon destroyed and both AP and HE delay [anti-personnel and high explosive shells] put through the slit at 2,000 yards.

Meanwhile, the Belgian Troop renewed the advance south of Black Hut, yet another bunker complex on the dunes. A Section immediately encountered a minefield and came under machine-gun fire as they tried to find a way round. Lieutenant Adolphe Meny was killed immediately, leaving Lieutenant Boris Artemieff to take the lead. Running forward, Artemieff was hit twice in the shoulder but still managed to silence one nest with his Tommy gun. Captain Danloy ordered Lieutenant Pierre Roman to outflank the strong point pinning down A Section. Distracted by the threat to their flank, the Germans failed to stop the HQ section's charge. Faced with the bayonet, four machine-gun posts surrendered, clearing the main German line of resistance. Eight Belgian Commandos were awarded the Croix de Guerre for their part in the action.

Captain Danloy ordered Lieutenant Roman to occupy the dunes north of the woods with a fighting patrol before the Germans recovered. The dunes were cleared easily, but Roman found his position dominated by an area of high ground. With Danloy's permission, Roman ordered his men forward:

> ... this small battle was an absolute classic of determination to get through at all costs and obtain one's objective, and, after the objective had been taken, to appreciate the situation and realise that something further must be done in order to make the position tenable.

There is no doubt that Lieutenant Roman's initiative and courage considerably speeded up the final outcome of the battle. He received the Military Cross for his actions:

> [Roman] showed a complete disregard for his personal safety and by his fine qualities of leadership and courage, he set a splendid example to the men under his command.

Meanwhile, 6 November was a momentous day on the Westkapelle beach. Previous attempts to land supplies had been aborted due to poor sea conditions but for once the weather relented sufficiently to attempt a landing. Rough seas caused one LCT to broach on the beach and its cargo was lost but the two remaining craft managed to land badly needed supplies

The exposed encampment on Green Beach, Westkapelle. H Houterman

and transport. 4 Special Service Brigade's wounded and some of the prisoners were evacuated on the return journey, after spending days on the exposed beach.

As 41 Commando had lost the majority of its transport in the initial landing, Brigadier Leicester had arranged for 4 Commando's to be transferred from Ostend. Although eighteen Weasels landed safely on White Beach, they were left on the south side of the gap by mistake. Attempts to transfer them across the gap nearly ended in tragedy:

The high seas and swift current tossed the small amphibians about like straws, and five Weasels were swamped and lost in the crossing. LVT crews came to the rescue of the drivers, and after a violent battle with the floods all of them were brought safely ashore.

Nine eventually reached Domburg, providing a valuable service. They worked day and night to ferry stores and wounded along the coast road.

The attack on 7 November benefited from a host of supportive fire. Mortars from three commandos had been gathered together and for once the weather relented, allowing effective air support. Eighteen Typhoons targeted the German positions around Black Hut and W19 with their canons and rockets as the marines moved into position. 41 Commando managed to reach the Black Hut position supported by two Shermans and once again the German *Kreigsmarine* had no stomach for close-quarter fighting. While the prisoners were led away the tank crews of 1st Lothian's inspected their handiwork:

... two Nebelwerfers were found destroyed in the spot at which we had been firing and a 50mm in a big emplacement. There was a hole in the gun, the marks of two HEs on the far wall and plenty of blood on the floor. A number of other pillboxes which had been engaged were badly knocked about.

Lieutenant-Colonel Palmer allowed his men to continue the advance in the hope of reaching W19 before dark. However, A Troop found the battery protected by an anti-tank ditch and a minefield. Machine-guns and mortars targeted the commandos as they ran for cover, wounding a dozen men in a matter of minutes. Lieutenant-Colonel Palmer ordered his men back to safety and while as Captain John Lash organised the evacuation of casualties, Typhoons strafed the woods north of Overduin to cover the withdrawal.

The Norwegian Troop, now led by Lieutenant Olav Gausland, had been progressing slowly through the woods. Engineers struggled to make a road forward through the minefields for the single remaining AVRE tank and after only 300 disaster struck. A mine ripped through the floor of the tank, mortally wounding three of the crew. The Norwegians would have to continue alone. Dozens of prisoners were taken and one volunteered some interesting information during his interrogation. The officer commanding W19 had decided to evacuate his position, drawing up a defensive line through the woods to face the developing threat. It meant that the weight of supporting fire gathering in support of 41 and 10 Commando could be put to good use.

The Final Surrender

The net had begun to close on the Germans trapped around Overduin and Vrouwenpolder. 4 Commando arrived in the area overnight, taking responsibility for the inland section from 10 Commando. The marines formed up and watched as the Canadian artillery gathered on the eastern edge of the island began targeting the woods at first light. They were gratified to see their objective shelled mercilessly, with virtually no reply.

At first light, 41 Commando was still trying to negotiate the minefield covering W19 on the dunes. Contrary to the prisoner's information, men could be seen manning the earthworks surrounding the battery. Palmer was concerned that he could be held up for another day and ordered B Troop to rush the minefield while P Troop provided covering fire. The attack took the Germans completely by surprise and before long white flags appeared outside every bunker.

4 Commando advanced cautiously through the woods, taking dozens of prisoners. Many freely admitting that

Lieutenant Kenneth Wright.

152

they had no prepared line and it appeared that they had been left to fend for themselves. As Lieutenant-Colonel Dawson monitored the progress through the woods inland, his staff were alarmed to see four armed Germans walk into their headquarters area. At first they thought the men had surrendered, but it soon became clear that they had been sent to arrange a formal surrender for all troops in the area. Under escort, the four took Lieutenant Kenneth Wright, 4 Commando's intelligence officer, to a nearby dugout. Following a brief telephone conversation with *Oberstleutnant* Wilhelm Veigele, 1020th Grenadier Regiment's commanding officer, transport was sent to collect Lieutenant-Colonel Dawson. Meanwhile, a cease-fire was ordered, and impending air strikes and artillery shoots were cancelled.

At 8:45 am the people of Vrouwenpolder were surprised to

Oberstleutnant William Veigele.

see a German staff car drive into the village with a British officer in the back seat and another perched on the bonnet. At first they did not know whether to cheer or remain silent. However, the smiles on the officers' faces soon convinced the locals that all was well. As the Dutch waved on, Lieutenant-Colonel Dawson and Lieutenant Wright arrived outside the German headquarters where *Oberstleutnant* Veigele waited with his staff. After formal salutes, the locals watched anxiously as the party stepped inside.

As Dawson negotiated surrender terms, outside events nearly cut short the meeting. The lead troops of 41 Commando had continued to advance along the dunes opening fire as they approached a strong point known as 'Fujiyama'. Although Veigele was unhappy about the breach in the cease-fire, several delicate phone calls restored the truce.

After finally agreeing terms, the two commanding officers made speeches in front of thirty-five German officers and as he handed over his weapon, Veigele explained with tears in his eyes how his disorganised men could not fight on without ammunition. Outside in the street, 4 Commando had confined

The final surrender. H Houterman

Prisoners in a make-shift camp wait to be evacuated.

the Dutch to their houses while they rounded up the prisoners and to avoid potential trouble. As the young commandos reflected on all they had seen over the past week, they watched as over 900 Germans said farewell to their officers. It was a civilised end to a battle in which all men had suffered terribly. By 1:00 pm Vrouwenpolder was virtually deserted, only a few German doctors and medical orderlies remained behind to tend the wounded.

Even though human opposition had ended, the island was still extremely dangerous. During the afternoon, Lieutenant-Colonel Moulton sent Captain Flunder and A Troop through the floods to meet 52nd Division in de Veere. As the two Buffaloes negotiated the road through Serooskerke, the second vehicle struck a huge mine. Twenty men were killed and nine injured in the explosion, (fifteen of the dead were marines of 48 Commando, its greatest loss of life since the landing).

Although the battle was over, bad weather prevented the commandos leaving Walcheren. For over a week they had to watch over their prisoners while arrangements were made to evacuate them. In the meantime stray Germans continued to give themselves up. 4 Commando's report relates how one incident amused the men:

> One such [German] *knocked on the door of a troop billet one night and asked meekly if he might surrender now that the danger was all over, as he had been too frightened to come out and do so before.*

Aftermath

With the island free, work could begin on clearing the Schelde estuary. For the next three weeks over a hundred minesweepers tirelessly swept the narrow channel, while navy

Minesweepers clearing the approaches to Antwerp.

divers worked hard to make Antwerp docks safe from explosives. Although they had been driven back from the Schelde, the Germans still tried to deny the port from the Allies. Throughout November over one hundred V2 rockets rained down on the city.

Finally, on 26 November three coasters berthed in the docks,

The estuary was clear and the passage to Antwerp was open.

Supplies for the civilian population as well as the fighting forces began to arrive.

the first of many. The Canadian liberty ship, *Fort Cataraqui*, docked two days later having led a convoy of ships up the estuary. They brought food and supplies for the starving Dutch, for although the occupation was over, it was only the start of a long hard winter.

The importance of 4 Special Service Brigade and 155 Infantry Brigade's efforts were highlighted three weeks later, when Hitler launched the Ardennes Offensive. In the battle that followed, huge quantities of supplies were lost and without Antwerp to restock the losses the war could have been prolonged for months.

Chapter Eleven

TOURING WALCHEREN

Vlissingen (Flushing)

Whichever route brought you to Vlissingen, from the outskirts of the town follow signs for *Centrum*. There are also signs for the *Arsenaal*, which stands alongside the old harbour close to the start point of your visit. There is plenty of street parking close to the harbour controlled by parking meters. Typically parking costs about 0.9 Euros (about 50 pence) an hour. Three or four hours should cover your visit to the town.

To start your tour of Flushing you need to locate Bellamypark, an open space in the centre of the old town overlooking the original harbour. The park is sign posted from many different locations and all the locals know it as the focal point of their town. The town has a one way system, which leads through the park and down to the harbour. Many of the streets around the old part of the town have on street parking, costing around one Euro an hour.

The Breskens Ferry

Until the end of 2002, visitors to Flushing made use of a regular car ferry. However, the completion of a new road tunnel under the River Schelde has made the crossing obsolescent. A smaller ferry, catering for foot passengers and cyclists, has replaced the service

Flushing seafront in November 1944. Hans Houterman

between Breksens and Flushing. The round trip takes about forty minutes (return cost about £1.50 in 2002). If time permits it is well worth making the trip, if only for spectacular views of the estuary and Walcheren. To locate the ferry follow signs for the railway station. There is ample parking nearby; the access to the ferry is opposite the station entrance.

Once onboard the ferry there is a little time to study the docks from the port side. Needless to say, the area has been considerably modernised, however, the layout of the keys has hardly changed since Scottish troops fought a running battle through the maze of quay side buildings and bunkers.

As the ferry swings out of the docks, it is possible to make out the remains of a bunker to the left of the entrance, the only coastal casemate to survive. Just beyond the bunker, partially obscured trees and undergrowth is Fort Rammekens. The Germans sited a gun battery, codenamed W6, on the roof of the fort to protect the harbour entrance.

From the ferry it is possible to obtain a unique view of the town, Uncle Beach was just to the right of the windmill, a prominent landmark during the landing. The entrance to the harbour and the old town also can be seen, overshadowed by the modern flats.

Breskens harbour is little more than two breakwaters, very much as it was in 1944. During the hours leading up to the assault, the area was a hive of activity as 4 Commando filed onto their landing craft.

While approaching Breskens there is time to briefly consider the fighting that went on the south side of the River Scheldt.

The Breskens Pocket

By 1944 the Germans had fortified Breskens and the area to the south. Recognising the importance of the port of Antwerp, Hitler was determined to deny its use from the Allies for as long as possible. Using the natural defence line of the Leopold Canal, which runs in an arc some ten miles inland, they had created a formidable defensive position. The area was cut off in September 1944, following the collapse of the Fifteenth German Army. From then on the Allies referred to the area as the Breskens Pocket. The Germans gave it a more sinister name, *Festung Schelde-Süd*, the South Scheldt Fortress. Many retreating units made their way through Breskens, escaping via Walcheren to the Dutch mainland. However, the 64th Infantry Division (many of the men were veterans of the Russian Front, recalled

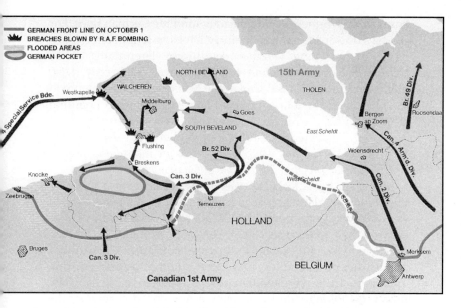

Legend:
- GERMAN FRONT LINE ON OCTOBER 1
- BREACHES BLOWN BY R.A.F. BOMBING
- FLOODED AREAS
- GERMAN POCKET

from leave) remained behind, with orders to hold the south bank of the River Scheldt.

Although 64th Division was cut off with no hope of escape, it showed no signs of surrender. Hitler's order to flood the area to aid defence had been carried out to the word, turning the area either side of the canal into a morass. What little land remained above water was littered with mines, while the flooded fields provided no cover from an alert enemy sniper or machine-gun post. It was going to be a bitter contest of wills.

On the morning of 6 October, the 3rd Canadian Infantry Division, launched assault boats across the Leopold Canal south of Eede. Although flame-throwing Bren-carriers managed to subdue the Germans, the Canadians became pinned to the canal bank. They were trapped, unable to link up the two small footholds on the canal bank. For the next forty-eight hours the Canadians tried to find a way through the maze of dikes, half wading, half swimming to make progress. On 9 October, the engineers finally bridged the canal bringing some hope to the troops trapped on the far bank.

Meanwhile, Lieutenant-General Simmonds had been looking for a way to outflank the position. During the early hours of the 9th, the 9th Canadian Infantry Brigade managed to cross the Savojaardsplaat inlet on the east side of the pocket. Within a few hours, it had formed a bridgehead behind the German lines. For six days, the 3rd Canadian Infantry Division fought a ferocious battle in appalling weather conditions. Eventually on 13 October the first Canadian troops entered Eede, only 1,000 metres from the Leopold Canal, the first dry land the men had seen for days. The following day Major-General Knut Eberding issued a severe warning to his men. Any man seen surrendering would be considered a deserter, and in Eberding's own words:

In cases where the names of deserters are ascertained these will be made known to the civilian population at home and their next of kin will be looked upon as enemies of the German people.

Eberding's words struck deep into the hearts of his men and at each dike or strong point, the Canadians were forced to kill or overrun their adversaries. Finally on the morning of 21 October, Breskens was in reach. Following concentrated artillery bombardments, bombing and close support by rocket-firing Typhoons, the first Canadian troops entered Breskens. They found a smoking ruin manned by a few dazed survivors; the rest had withdrawn to new positions.

Cornered and running low on ammunition, Eberding's men fought on to the last. Some fought on for another four days in Fort Frederik Hedrik, an ancient coastal defensive work to the north-west of Breskens. On the morning of the 26th, fifty dazed prisoners finally gave themselves up. With the southern coast of the estuary cleared, the engineers could now work on clearing Breskens harbour in preparation for Operation INFATUATE.

Even so, the battle for the pocket was far from over. A few Germans were pushed into a tiny pocket east of Breskens, and eventually on 1 November, a subdued Major-General Eberding was finally captured. Fighting also continued around Retranchment and Sluis until finally, on 3 November General Simmonds could announce that the pocket was cleared. Over 12,500 prisoners were finally counted. An operation expected to last four days had taken over four weeks to complete.

The return journey across the estuary follows the same route the commandos and Scots took, turning close to the shore to make its way into the docks. There is also ample time to study the coastline north of Flushing. If the visibility is allows it is possible to see Westkapelle Lighthouse the focal point of Operation INFATUATE II.

Flushing, the view from the Breskens Ferry.

ORANGE MILL   UNCLE BEACH

Walking Tour 1

Flushing: The landing - *30 minutes*

Starting from Bellamy Park, **(1)** walk onto the small promontory, separating the two harbours. The De Ruyter statue stands high up on the promontory to the right. The Arsenal, (Arsenaal in Dutch) a large brick built building once used as a German barracks, overlooks the harbour; ironically it has now used as a children's

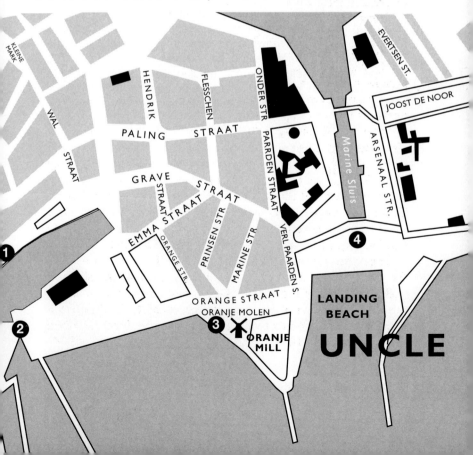

Bellamy Park, codenamed 'Braemar'.

activity centre. At the end of the promontory **(2)** climb the steps onto the small swing bridges to cross the entrance of the harbour. If the swing bridges are closed, or steps present a problem, follow the perimeter of the harbour to the entrance of the Arsenal.

Once on the foreshore, head east towards Oranje Molen **(3)**, the Orange Windmill. On a clear day it is possible to see Breskens across the estuary, meanwhile the streets behind the dike, code named 'Seaford', were cleared by the first troops ashore. The windmill was a useful landmark, guiding the landing craft onto Uncle Beach. An entrance to a pillbox can be found on the seaward side of the windmill, built into the seawall. The pillbox has

The bunker at the foot of the Oranje Molen; the Orange Mill.

Looking west along Uncle Beach, the beach ran in line with the windmill in 1944. See pages 47 and 100.

been made safe in recent years and plans have been muted to turn it into a small museum in the near future.

Continue east along the dike to the site of Uncle Beach. Unfortunately, the area has changed a great deal since the war; improvement works have changed the alignment of the seawall, burying the original foreshore beneath the dike. In 1944 the beach consisted of a small inlet sheltered by two promontories and although it was the ideal place to land, Keepforce's assessment shows what the Commandos faced:

4 Commando and 155 Brigade's memorial near 'Uncle' Beach.

> *Obstacles consisting of three rows of stakes possibly mined, then a ditch anti-tank, then three rows of steel rails set in concrete at the top of a steep bank. Possibility of the beach having been sown with anti-personal and anti-tank mines.*

Make your way down one of the paths to 4 Commando's memorial **(4)** behind the dike. The statue forms the centrepiece of a small park and a plaque dedicated to the men of the 52nd (Lowland) Division stands alongside. Three battalions of 155

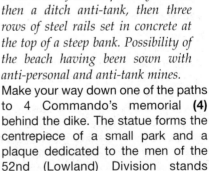

The old harbour, 'Brighton' pillbox forced 4 Commando to head into the town.

Brigade came ashore at Uncle beach on 1 November.

From the memorial head back towards the centre of the town, along Commandoweg, (Landingstraat is also nearby). Continue past the old Arsenal, on the right hand, and along Graavestraat, the route used by the commandos as they raced towards the town centre. A machine-gun post, next to De Ruyter's statue, opened fire across the harbour, forcing the lead troop to turn into Walstraat. Follow their tracks, taking the first left into Nieuwstraat. The street has changed little since the war and it is quite easy to visualise the commandos moving forward at the double. Bellamypark at the top of the street marks the end of the first walk around the town.

As the lead troops cleared the buildings around the park, those following headed down the streets on the far side. Heavy fighting took place in the area overlooked by the modern flats and the area had to be completely rebuilt after the war. The flats run along the seafront and their predecessors were used as naval barracks during the war.

Walking Tour 2

Flushing: The battle continues - *60 minutes*

Bellamypark provides the starting point for the next tour of the town. Take the narrow street at the north-east corner of the park, Kerkstraat, heading for the church tower. St Jacob's Church witnessed a moving memorial service on 11 November 1944. Several hundred soldiers and locals gathered together to remember those killed during the liberation of the island. The church still acts as the focal point for commemorative services and each anniversary pipe bands gather in the town to entertain the crowds of veterans and locals who gather to enjoy the spectacle.

Keeping to the left of the church head through the shops along Vrouwestraat and after a short distance, turn left into Walstraat. The shops lining the main street have been completely rebuilt, although many of the side streets look as they did in 1944. There are a wide selection of shops, cafes and restaurants in this part of the town, and it is an ideal place to purchase postcards or snacks.

Continue to the end of Walstraat, past the charming water feature, to Betje Wolfplein crossroads. **(1)** The junction was code named 'Bexhill', were some of the fiercest fighting took place. Although many of the buildings around the crossroads have changed, it is possible to follow the battle for this important road

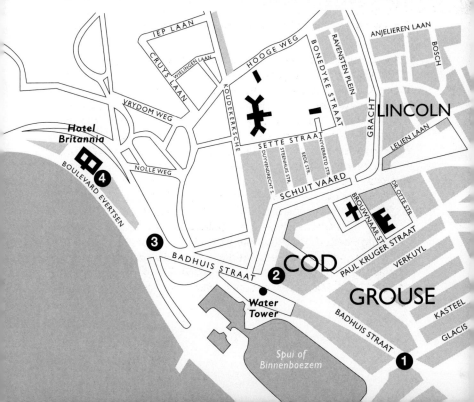

DOVER
PILLBOX

Looking west from 'Bexhill' along Goosje Buskenstraat.

Aagje Dekenstraat runs east from 'Bexhill' crossroads.

MG POST

DOCKYARD
GATES

junction. 'Dover', the pillbox that caused so many casualties, was at the end of the road to the left, Coosje Buskenstraat. In 1944 the gates of the De Schelde Shipyard stood on the site of the large retail store to the right. A machine-gun post along Aagje Dekenstraat prevented any movement down in that direction.

A few commandos managed to cross the junction before daylight on 1 November 1944 and they were able to prevent German reinforcements entering the town. The sounds of battle quickly alerted the German posts covering the junction, preventing any more troops crossing. The following morning the 5th KOSBs crossed the junction in force at first light, covered by smoke. As the Scots progressed into the New Town, hundreds of civilians crossed Aagje Dekenstraat in the opposite direction into the shipyard where waiting soldiers escorted them to safety.

The view north from 'Bexhill', otherwise known as Hellfire Corner.

Cross over the junction and head straight forward along Badhuisstraat, following the route of the 5th KOSBs. Mortar fire targeted the forming up area as they prepared to clear the streets to the right, code named 'Grouse', 'Pike' and 'Partridge' and in

The Royal Scots were pinned down on the embankment, with Germans to their front and rear.

spite of heavy casualties, the Scots set about their task. The area east of Badhuisstraat suffered a great deal of damage during the battle and had to be completely rebuilt after the war.

Continue along the tree-lined avenue, known as 'Cod', passing the defunct town hall on the right.

On the night of 2 November 1944 the 7/9th Royal Scots advanced along Badhuisstraat heading for the Grand Hotel Britannia. The lead elements came under machine-gun fire from

The Royal Scots ran across the road under fire to reach the back of the hotel.

the water tower along the road, on the left **(2)**. After clearing the tower, the Royal Scots were forced to take cover while they were subjected to 'friendly fire'. By the time the bombardment finished the flood waters had risen to alarming depths.

Go straight across the crossroads past the foot of the water tower, heading along the tree lined avenue. The floods continued to rise as the Royal Scots made their way forward and at times the soldiers were chest deep in freezing sea water. Although the Scots headed right along Vrydomweg, our route is straight on. Follow the road, Burgemeester van Woelderenlaan, turning right at the foot an impressive flight of steps **(3)** and continue along the foot of embankment. The hotels lining the sea front can be seen to your left above the trees.

Stop 250 metres from the steps, where Bakkersdorplaan joins from the right. The Grand Hotel Britannia is at the top of the embankment, and the Royal Scots approached their objective through the houses, stumbling on a pillbox at the foot of the slope. Although the bunker was taken following a brief fire-fight, the noise alerted the Germans guarding the hotel. Under fire, the Royals ran forward to take cover in the dead ground at the foot of the slope.

Climb the steps to the top of the embankment and the Grand Britannia Hotel is directly in front **(4)**. There have been considerable changes in this area; the original building was badly damaged during the battle and the replacement building is scheduled for demolition.

Lieutenants George and Cameron led two parties across the road through a gauntlet of fire to reach the hotel while the rest of the battalion remained pinned down on the embankment. After a time, the building was set on fire, forcing the Royal Scots to seek refuge in the network of trenches lining the road. A flak cannon on the roof of the German headquarters (the hotel south of the Britannia) was silenced when Lieutenant Beveridge scaled the outer wall of the building. *Oberst* Reinhardt and his staff were eventually discovered in an underground bunker. The Royal Scots charged the hotel buildings after their leader, Lieutenant-Colonel Melvill, fell wounded; over 600 Germans capitulated in the face of the frenzied assault.

Turning right walk along the rear of several hotels until you reach the promenade. If time permits you may wish to head towards the German bunker on the seafront, to take in views of the Schelde.

DOVER PILLBOX

MARTELLO TOWER

Flushing seafront in 2002, compare with the scene on page 48.

The walk back to the old town gives time to reflect on the events that took place in Flushing back in November 1944.

Ahead, approximately 600 metres away, a tall steel obelisk stands at the end of Coosje Buskenstraat on the site of 'Dover' pillbox. From the foot of the tower it is possible to see how important the position was, dominating the both the seafront and Bexhill junction. 4 Commando fought tenaciously to reach the bunker, 'mouseholing' along either side of Coosje Buskenstraat.

Continue along the sea wall to a defensive work from a different era. The Martello tower, a watchtower from the renaissance era, has stood guard over the estuary for more than three hundred

'Dover' pillbox dominated Goosje Buskenstraat.

BEXHILL CROSSROADS

Admiral De Ruyter's memorial.

years; it now provides cover for a restaurant. The original flats opposite the tower were the German barracks code named 'Worthing'; 'Hove' was a little further along, where the promenade turns east.

A memorial to one of Walcheren's heroes stands at the end of the promenade. In June 1667 De Rutyer led the Dutch fleet up the River Thames and over the course of three days his men burnt a large number of capital warships, crippling the English Navy. De Rutyer led his victorious fleet back to Amsterdam with two capital ships in tow. In Evelyn's words: 'a dreadful spectacle as ever Englishmen saw and a dishonour never to be wiped off!' The attack placed London in a state of panic, and within weeks the England had signed the Peace of Breda.

Return to your vehicle to visit the rest of the island.

The road to Dishoek

Follow the one way system around Bellamypark, and **leave the park via Spuistraat** and the opposite end to the harbour. Drive straight ahead at the traffic lights, crossing Coosje Buskenstraat. **Turn left at the crossroads** on to Badhuisstraat, by the water-tower and follow the road as it swings right at the foot of the ornamental steps. Head along Burgemeester van Woelderenlaan behind the Britannia hotel and continue **straight on at the traffic lights**.

After a mile go **straight on at the roundabout**. Two bunkers in the fields, right of the road, give some idea how formidable the German defensive positions were. These specimens were rendered useless by the flooding. W4, the last bastion of defence on this part of the island, once stood on the high dunes to the left. It fell to 47 Royal Marine Commando on 3 November, finally linking the Flushing and Westkapelle beachheads.

Turn left, sign posted for Dishoek, following the road as it turns sharp right at the foot of the dunes. At the far end of the village, there is a large car park on the right, Your stay in Dishoek will only be short, so in quiet times you may wish to find a free place to park.

W11, the Dishoek Battery – *20 minutes*

The road turns sharp left a few yards beyond the entrance to the car park, in front of a cycle hire shop. Follow the steep path to the top of the dunes and at the top, when the sea comes into view, take the path to the left. After a short distance take the short flight of steps on the right.

There is a useful orientation platform at the top and it stands at the centre of the Dishoek Battery. On a clear day it is possible to see Zoutelande and Westkapelle to the north west and Flushing to the south east and on 2 November 47 Commando advanced towards the battery from the direction of Zoutelande.

The commandos were hemmed in by water on both sides limiting the marines to a frontal attack. Their first attack took the dune to the north, where there is now a small lighthouse tower. 47 Commando were pinned down for several hours as they tried to cross the gully in front, suffering heavy casualties. A final charge after dusk managed to capture many of the casemates but Lieutenant-Colonel Phillips was forced to order a withdrawal, having lost so many officers and men. 47 Commando renewed the advance the following morning, crossing the gully and clearing the battery.

Return to the foot of the dunes and head back into the village. Turn left onto the footpath in front of the cycle shop to visit Dishoek

The German perspective of 47 Commando's approach to Dishoek.

ZOUTELANDE

SEARCHLIGHT

GULLY

church (a white square building, almost Middle Eastern in appearance). The church is only a short distance away, on the right, and simple plaque by the door lists 47 Commando's roll of honour.

Zoutelande

Return to your vehicle and **retrace your route** through the village, **turning left onto Zwaanweg**. After half a mile, **turn right at the roundabout** sign posted Koudekerke. **Turn left at the T junction** another half a mile further on and as you head towards Zoutelande take note of the bunkers. **Turn sharp left** in front of the dunes, at the far end of the village; the church is on the left and there is limited parking nearby.

Zoutelande was liberated at 11:00am on 2 November by A Troop of 48 Commando and a plaque on the church wall remembers the occasion. As Captain Daniel Flunder celebrated with the mayor, a misguided shell from HMS *Erebus* crashed through the roof of the church. The second memorial remembers those who died during the period of occupation; the inscription reads *'out of the darkest valley into the light'*. On 5 November 1944 48 and 47 Commandos joined the local population in service of thanksgiving in the ruined church.

Climb the steps opposite the church to visit the sea front. In 1944 the commandos cleared the bunkers which lined the beach, eventually establishing a position on the high dunes to the south. Head along the promenade towards the dunes to visit a new museum (it is only open Wednesday and Sunday afternoons, but

Entrance to the Bunker Museum.

Looking north west from the second of the museum's bunkers.

still worth a visit if closed). Two small German bunkers have been restored and the first is located on the inland face of the dike behind Hotel Tien Torens. Examples of German beach obstacles guard the entrance and the bunker has been equipped as it was during the war and there are numerous photographs depicting life in Zoutelande between 1940 and 1944. Follow the path behind the accommodation bunker to reach the second bunker on the highest dune. The observation dome could see for miles around and you can still see other large bunkers hidden in the undergrowth on the slopes below it.

The twin lighthouse towers, close to the site of the Dishoek battery, can be seen to the south-east, but much nearer, (difficult to see with the naked eye, barely accessible and hard to find) a

Westkapelle lighthouse.

solitary cross stands on top of a high dune. It remembers six local men executed for sabotage in that isolated place back in September 1944.

As you return to your car you can see Westkapelle along the coast to the north west. You may wish to take advantage of the shops and cafés along the high street; a small supermarket sells most types of provisions.

Westkapelle Lighthouse and Cemetery

Return to main road, **turning left for Westkapelle** and as the road winds its way behind the dunes Westkapelle lighthouse can be seen ahead on the horizon. At the foot of the lighthouse, where the main road turns sharp left into the village, **turn right** (actually heading straight ahead) onto the side road. Park on the right a few yards from the junction. A simple cross stands at the centre of a semicircle of graves behind the lighthouse. The small cemetery remembers the inhabitants of Westkapelle killed during the Allied bombing and the battle that followed.

175 civilians perished, forty-seven of them trapped by rising floodwater in the ruins of *De Roos Molen* (Rose Mill). Mr and Mrs Theune, the elderly couple who owned the **Remembering those** mill are buried near the foot of the cross. **who died during the** Entire families were lost in the tragedy and **occupation** forty-three children who died in the flooding are buried alongside their parents. A memorial stone remembers sixteen men, women and children whose bodies were never found.

4 Special Service Brigade

Landings at Westkapelle – *45 minutes*

Return to your car and find a safe place to **turn round. Turn right** at the main road and follow the tree-lined avenue through the village. The bombing and subsequent floods completely destroyed Westkapelle and it took many years to rebuild the village. A plaque on the village hall, laid by T Force's commanding officer Commander Pugsley, commemorates the regeneration works. Continue along the main street and follow it as it turns right at the foot of the dike, there is a small car park a short distance along the road. **(1)**

Climb the steps to the top of the dike and make your way to the Sherman tank. The tank stands on the site of Hedrik Mill, destroyed in the bombing raids. Rose Mill, where forty-three people drowned, stood at the foot of the dike.

The memorial **(2)** is a good place to study how Operation INFATUATE II developed. Bombing created a large gap in the dunes and the line of the original dike juts out into the sea, pointing towards the radar station. Red Beach was immediately north of the memorial.

The first wave of 41 Commando managed to land on the beach, occupying the crest of the dike. W15 battery, a line of casements lining the top of the dike, was half a mile north of the memorial. British engineers destroyed the bunkers after the battle. The guns initially engaged the landing craft of the Support Squadron, as they drew fire from the landing craft. 41

177

Westkapelle's memorial to the landings on 1 November

Commando advanced along the foot of the dike once the village had been cleared, capturing the battery.

The majority of the landing craft came ashore on White Beach. After sailing through the gap the rest of 41 Commando, followed by 10 Commando, landed on the northern flank of the dike. They advanced into the village heading for the lighthouse, while tanks climbed onto the dike to give supporting fire. 48 Commando beached on the southern flank of the gap, in front of the Radar Station.

There are two ways of getting to the radar station on the opposite side of the gap. Either take the wooden walkway across the beach, or follow the wide promenade that loops behind the new section of dike.

Two memorials, remembering the Support Squadron and 4 Special Service Brigade, stand close to the radar station **(3)**. Green

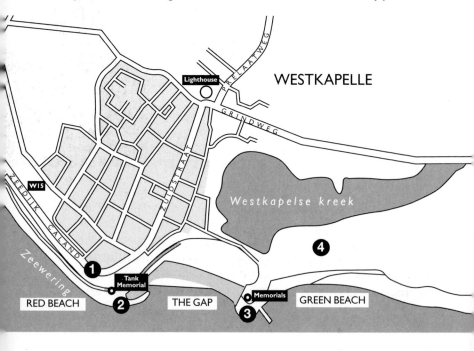

Beach, the area used to land supplies, was to the south. If you are feeling energetic, it is well worth climbing the steps behind the radar station to visit a useful orientation table,**(4)** affording astounding views of the landing beaches. After clearing the bunkers covering the beaches, 48 Commando headed south, past Green Beach, towards W13 Battery.

Follow the path running behind the new dike to return to your vehicle. After the war, Dutch engineers closed the gap with block ships, forming a new sea wall on the inland side. As you walk back along the dike, take time to reflect on the devastation caused and the sacrifices made by civilians and soldiers during the autumn of 1944.

Domburg - *45 minutes*

Head **north on the main road** behind the dike, Domburg is four miles away. 41 Commando trudged along the dunes on the afternoon of 1 November, heading for the Domburg battery. The bunkers disappeared many years ago and the site is now occupied by golf links, (many of the shell craters made by the Bombardment Squadron were turned into bunkers). Continue into Domburg along Schelpweg following the one way system through the village, as the road turns right, following the signpost for Centre. You can leave you vehicle in the car park behind the Tourist Information Centre on the left.

Turning left onto the main road, take the first left, Stationstraat; Domburg church is at the end. Turn right and walk along the main street, through the busy shopping centre.

41 Commando entered Domburg late on 1 November but it was unable to secure the village before 10 (Inter-Allied) Commando arrived the following day. The arrival of Major Pocock and his four remaining tanks turned the tide and by nightfall on 2 November Domburg was clear.

Domburg's water tower still bears its scars from the battle.

Turn left onto Badstraat at the crossroads, behind the Bad Hotel; the sea front is a few minutes walk away.

On the promenade, take note of the small memorial dedicated to the Belgian troop of 10 (Inter-Allied) Commando to the left. Turning right, head along the path towards the water tower. The damage

Exposed dunes and thick woods in the Black Hut area

made by Pocock's tanks can be clearly seen. If time permits, the walk along the front is well worth making. It is possible to locate the position of W18, the flak position taken by 41 Commando. It stood on the highest dune, half a mile east of the village. The bunkers were demolished years ago but there are traces of concrete and brick scattered around the location. The walk to W18 allows time to study the terrain east of Domburg. While 41 Commando moved cautiously along the exposed dunes, 10 Commando fought its way through the woods.

Return along the sea front and through Domburg to your vehicle.

Black Hut – *30 minutes*

Turning **left out of the car park**, follow the one way system through Domburg. After a short distance the main road turns sharp left, then right onto Domburgseweg, in front of Bad Hotel. The road heads east through the woods to Oostkapelle, two miles away. **Turn left** into Waterstraat in front of Oostkapelle church and after a quarter of a mile, bear left into Duinstraat at a mini-roundabout. Head north through the woods cleared by 10 (Inter-Allied) Commando, holiday homes now line the road. There is a small car park at the foot of the dunes. Note that the area is a nature reserve, so keep to the marked paths.

Follow the footpath onto the dunes, to the site of Black Hut (a café now stands on the beach). The entire north coast of the island can be seen from the top of the dike, starting with Domburg water tower to the west. While 41 Commando advanced along the dunes supported by two Shermans, the Belgian and Norwegian troops of 10 Commando fought snipers in the woods. W19 battery stood on the dunes to the east. As the commandos closed in most of the garrison fled into the woods.

After studying the landscape, return to your car.

Vrouwenpolder

Heading back into Oostkapelle, bear left at the mini roundabout and follow the road out of the village. Serooskerke is two miles further on. If time permits, **turn left** half a mile beyond the village, heading north to Vrouwenpolder. Otherwise continue south towards Middelburg; the Abbey Tower makes an ideal landmark.

As you approach the village, prepare to **turn left** heading for the centre. There is a small memorial stone at the centre of a small green behind the church; it remembers the liberation of the village. The plaque depicts a hand strangling the German eagle and it was originally set above the door of the German headquarters. The stone was relocated in its current setting when the house was demolished in the 1970's. The local German officer surrendered with 900 men on the morning of 8 November, bringing the battle for the island to an end.

Vrowenpolder's liberation memorial.

Return to the junction south of Serooskerke, following signs for Middelburg. The town is only four miles from Vrouwenpolder.

Middelburg – *30 minutes*

There are a multitude of one way streets and pedestrian precincts in Middelburg but the town centre is fairly small and easy to find your way around on foot. Car parks, costing less than one Euro an hour or about 50p, surround the town.

Head for the fifteenth century town hall in the main square. There is a market on most days but on 6 November 1944, the square witnessed one of the most peculiar episodes of the Second World War.

Around 4:30pm in the afternoon, eight Buffaloes roared into the square and before long dozens of Germans began to crowd around the small number of Royal Scots, eager to surrender. The Germans thought that large armoured force had entered the town and by nightfall hundreds had congregated in the square. The Scots positioned a Buffalo at each corner of the square and members of the Dutch underground soon joined them on guard duty.

With your back to the town hall, take the street called Lange Deflt, in the far left corner. Damplien, the second square where several hundred German prisoners gathered, is at the end. Follow the buildings on the right hand side as you enter the square. A pair of white buildings numbered 6 and 8 Dam face the bandstand, and housed the German headquarters. Major Johnson negotiated the surrender of the town inside with the uncompromising General

Middelburg's magnificent town hall.

No 6 and No 8 Dam, General Daser's headquarters See page 141.

Daser. There is a small plaque on the wall commemorating the liberation of the town.

Retracing across the square you can either return to the town hall or visit the magnificent twelfth century Abbey, with its museum of local history. The Abbey tower, known as Lange Jan (Long John), rises 300 feet above the town.

Bergen-op-Zoom War Cemetery

Many of the war graves from Operation INFATUATE were originally dotted around Walcheren, close to where the men had died. However, after the war the Commonwealth War Graves Commission decided to concentrate dozens of burial grounds

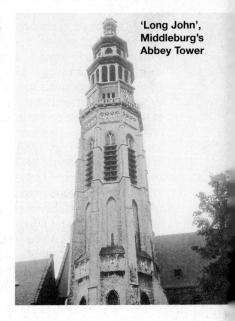

'Long John', Middleburg's Abbey Tower

183

and isolated graves around Zeeland into a central location. The decision meant that the Commission could maintain the graves at a reasonable cost. Unfortunately, many graves had to be moved considerable distances from their original location, including those who died on Walcheren. The cemetery was built at Bergen-op-Zoom, a central location linked by road and rail to the ports. Although a handful of casualties from the Support Squadron are buried at Bergen, many of the bodies were transported back to Ostend and buried in the communal cemetery. The soldiers with no known grave are remembered on memorials scattered far and wide. Missing Naval personnel are remembered on the Royal Naval memorials at their respective bases of Chatham, Portsmouth and Plymouth. The small number of missing Army personnel are remembered on the Groesbeek Memorial, east of Nijmegen.

To reach Bergen, take the **A58 motorway from Middelburg** or Vlissingen. The cemetery is a straightforward drive of forty miles and the journey should take approximately forty-five minutes. After bypassing Goes, the motorway passes beneath the Zuid Beveland Canal. Leave the A58 two miles after Bergen-op-Zoom, at Junction 26 (sign posted for Heerle). Turn left at the top of the slip road heading for Bergen-op-Zoom and after a few hundred metres turn left at the T-Junction, again following signs for Bergen-op-Zoom and Heerle. The road runs parallel with the motorway, bypassing a petrol station on the left after half a mile. The war cemetery stands among the trees to the right, half a mile further on.

Nearly 1,300 graves stand together in the peaceful woodland setting and half belong to airmen shot down over Zeeland and the surrounding provinces between 1944 and 1945. They were originally buried close to the crash site, either in a field or local cemetery. Flight Lieutenant Patrick Garland is buried in the first row of Plot IV. He died on New Year's Day 1945, the eldest of four pilot officer brothers killed on active service. His youngest brother, twenty-one year old Flying Officer Donald Garland VC, was killed in May 1940 leading a flying mission to destroy a vital bridge over the Albert Canal during the German Blitzkrieg.

The graves relating to Operation INFATUATE are scattered around the cemetery, intermingled with graves belonging to men killed during the liberation of South Beveland. The majority of the Walcheren graves can be found in Plot V and VI, just in front of the Cross of Sacrifice, others can be found in Plots XV, XVI and XXI beyond the pergolas. A shelter stands at the far end from the gate, where it is possible to sit and read the register or fill in the visitor's book.

The battlefield cemetery at 'Uncle' Beach. H Houterman

Bergen-op-Zoom War Cemetery.

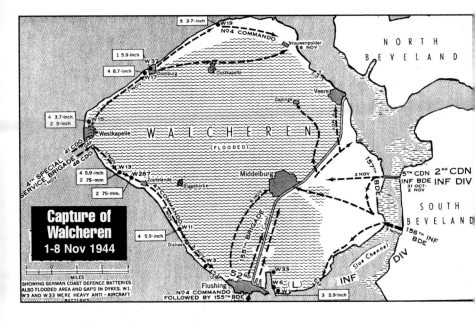

Major Derek de Stackpoole, killed during 48 Commando's battle for W13 is buried in Plot VI, Row B. He was the son of the 5th Duke of Stackpoole of County Meath. Lieutenant David Winser, 48 Commando's medical officer, is buried alongside. Winser had been a student at Corpus Christi College, Oxford before he joined the commandos, and rowed three times for his university. Nineteen-year-old Lieutenant Lindrea is buried close by. 41 Commando's officers were originally buried in Domburg cemetery but their graves are now scattered. Major 'Paddy' Brind-Sheridan is buried in Plot V, Row C, while, Captain Peter Haydon, Y Troop's commander, and Lieutenant John Holmes are buried together in Plot XV, Row B. Many of the Royal Scots killed during the attack on the Grand Hotel Britannia are buried together in Plot XXII. Major G Chater and Captain W Thompson are among them.

Bergen-op-Zoom Canadian War Cemetery is 200 metres to the west. Again there are around a 1,000 graves and as the name suggests, it is almost exclusively Canadian. The majority died in Operation VITALITY, the clearing of South Beveland.

After visiting the cemeteries, retrace your steps past the petrol station, and rejoin the A58 at Junction 26. Remember that the Dutch drive on the right and you need the first entrance onto the motorway, sign posted for Goes and Middelburg. There is time to reflect on the battle for the peninsula during the return journey to Walcheren. The 2nd Canadian Infantry Division advanced north from Antwerp on 4 October 1944 and Allied commanders expected to reach Walcheren in less than four days. They were to be bitterly disappointed.

For two weeks the Canadians fought against a determined force of German paratroops among dikes and flooded fields as they tried to seal off the South Beveland peninsula. The battles for Hoogerheide and Woensdrecht at the neck of the peninsula were particularly bloody and it took until the end of the month to overcome their opponents. The route west along the peninsula was narrow and protected by strongly held positions and minefields. Armour was unable to advance leaving the Canadian infantry to fight on alone. The deadlock was finally broken when the 52nd (Lowland) Division carried out an amphibious landing at Hoedekenskerke outflanking strong positions along the Zuid Beveland Canal. As resistance collapsed, the Canadians swept through the town of Goes reaching the eastern edge of Walcheren. They were confronted with a narrow strip of land, the only way onto the island. For three days first the Canadians, then the Scots, fought a bitter battle to cross the Causeway. The deadlock was finally broken when Scottish troops crossed the mudflats surrounding the Sloe Channel at night. They eventually entered Middelburg during the early hours of 6 November, relieving the Royal Scots.

INDEX

119, 120, 153
Moyes, Capt, 123

Nahuÿs, H van, 55
Nauta, E, 135
Newton-Dunn, Maj T, 142, 144, 145
Nisbet, 2nd Lt, 98
Nuttall, Capt T, 92

Oakeshott, A, 79, 89
Orum, Lt S, 68

Palmer, Lt-Col, E, 81, 86, 87, 89, 90, 94, 96, 126, 148, 149, 151, 152
Penney, Capt G, 71, 73
Phillips, Lt-Col, F 87, 88, 119, 121-126, 174
Place, Lt E, 98
Pocock, Maj D, 127, 128, 179, 180
Prior, Cmdr R, 85
Pugsley, Captain A, DSO, RN, 37, 63, 65, 177

Rasmussen, Lt R, 66
Reinhardt, Oberst W, 25, 103, 114, 116, 171
Rewcastle, Captain D, 45
Ring, Lt G, RNR, 68
Roman, Lt P, 126, 149, 150
Rose, Major H, 108-115
Rose, Lt-Col R, 146

Sellar, Captain K, DSC, RN, 37, 39, 66, 70, 77, 91
Sendall, Major W, 84, 92
Senée, Lt J, 55
Simmonds, General, 18, 36, 161-162
Skelton, Capt, 91

Smith, Sub-Lt J, 68
Spencer, Capt, 123-125
Square, Lt J, 92
Stacpoole, Major D de, 90, 186

Terwoert, M, 135
Theune family, 28, 177
Thomson, Lt, 121
Thomson, Capt G, 108, 114
Thorburn, Capt A, 46, 101, 103
Tiplady, Lt E, 72
Tullett, Lt E, 98
Turner, Lt-Col W, 60, 97, 101, 130-132

Vernon, Lt-Col S, RNVR, 36, 60
Veigele, Oberstleutant, 153
Vincent, Major, 122
Vourch, Capt G, 54-56

Ward, Lt M, 70
Wilks, Lt A, 76
Webb, Major G, 48, 51
Whitby, Lt-Comm J, 33
Widdowson, Lt J, 112, 115
Wilson, Capt J, 46
Winser, Lt D, MC, 81, 186
Winter, Lt, 125
Wood, Rev J, 110
Wood, Major P, 94
Wright, Lt K, 153

Places
Antwerp, 8, 15-18, 24, 157, 158, 160, 187
Breskens, 12, 18, 24, 35, 36, 43, 60, 159, 160, 162, 164
Bergen-op-Zoom, 8, 9, 18, 184-186
Chatham, 184
Dishoek, 26, 35, 105, 120-125, 173-174

Formations and Units
Allied Army

German